Cheerleading

Other titles in the Science Behind Sports series:

Cheerleading

HEATHER E. SCHWARTZ

LUCENT BOOKS
A part of Gale, Cengage Learning

GALE
CENGAGE Learning·

Detroit • New York • San Francisco • New Haven, Conn • Waterville, Maine • London

LIBRARY OF CONGRESS CATALOGING-IN-PUBLICATION DATA

Schwartz, Heather E.
  Cheerleading / Heather E. Schwartz.
    p. cm. -- (Science behind sports)
  Summary: "This series will present the science behind key contemporary sports. Each
title in the series will focus on one sport (or a group of related sports) that will give
readers an overview of the sport, scientific principles and concepts related to the sport,
biomechanics and physiology related to playing the sport, and relevant elements of
related sports medicine"-- Provided by publisher.
  Includes bibliographical references and index.
  ISBN 978-1-4205-0818-5 (hardback)
  1. Cheerleading--Juvenile literature. 2. Sports sciences--Juvenile literature.
  LB3635.S38 2012
  791.6'4--dc23
                                                                    2012004928

Lucent Books
27500 Drake Rd
Farmington Hills MI 48331

ISBN-13: 978-1-4205-0818-5
ISBN-10: 1-4205-0818-0

Printed in the United States of America

1 2 3 4 5 6 7 16 15 14 13 12

TABLE OF CONTENTS

On March 21, 1970, Slovenian ski jumper Vinko Bogataj took a terrible fall while competing at the Ski-flying World Championships in Oberstdorf, West Germany. Bogataj's pinwheeling crash was caught on tape by an ABC *Wide World of Sports* film crew and eventually became synonymous with "the agony of defeat" in competitive sporting. While many viewers were transfixed by the severity of Bogataj's accident, most were not aware of the biomechanical and environmental elements behind the skier's fall—heavy snow and wind conditions that made the ramp too fast and Bogataj's inability to maintain his center of gravity and slow himself down. Bogataj's accident illustrates that, no matter how mentally and physically prepared an athlete may be, scientific principles—such as momentum, gravity, friction, and aerodynamics—always have an impact on performance.

Lucent Book's Science Behind Sports series explores these and many more scientific principles behind some of the most popular team and individual sports, including baseball, hockey, gymnastics, wrestling, swimming, and skiing. Each volume in the series focuses on one sport or group of related sports. The volumes open with a brief look at the featured sport's origins, history and changes, then move on to cover the biomechanics and physiology of playing, related health and medical concerns, and the causes and treatment of sports-related injuries.

In addition to learning about the arc behind a curve ball, the impact of centripetal force on a figure skater, or how water buoyancy helps swimmers, Science Behind Sports readers will also learn how exercise, training, warming up, and diet and nutrition directly relate to peak performance and enjoyment of the sport. Volumes may also cover why certain sports are popular, how sports function in the business world, and which hot sporting issues—sports doping and cheating, for example—are in the news.

Basic physical science concepts, such as acceleration, kinetics, torque, and velocity, are explained in an engaging and accessible manner. The full-color text is augmented by fact boxes, sidebars, photos, and detailed diagrams, charts and graphs. In addition, a subject-specific glossary, bibliography and index provide further tools for researching the sports and concepts discussed throughout Science Behind Sports.

CHAPTER 1

Transformation of Cheerleading

Cheerleading is a popular and energetic activity that requires strength, special skills, creativity, and stamina. Like in many sports, athletes who perform in cheerleading need to rise to physical challenges, and they compete against other cheerleaders. Despite these similarities, there is a continuing debate over whether cheerleading is a sport or is simply an activity designed to cheer on other athletes when they compete.

Some say it is both, since today there are cheerleaders who perform on the sidelines of sporting events, such as football games and basketball games and those who compete against other cheerleaders in their own competitive events. In 2011, journalist Katie Thomas explored the questions for the *New York Times* newspaper, explaining that "while cheerleading evokes images of pompoms and pleated skirts, it has relied on increasingly athletic feats of grace and strength in recent years. As participants have perfected their basket tosses and pyramids, and mounted ambitious floor routines, a complicated and emotional question has arisen: has cheerleading become a true sport?"[1]

Over the years, the public impression of cheerleading has changed significantly. In part, this is because the nature of cheerleading has changed substantially since its creation in the mid-1800s. As cheerleading moved from the sidelines and became more competitive, it attracted its own fans, eager to be excited and energized by dazzling performances.

The Early Years of Cheerleading

In its earliest incarnation, cheerleading was an effort to get college sports spectators more excited and involved as they watched their teams play. It was thought that the spectators' energy could motivate a team to work harder to win. While cheering by the audience at games was nothing new, the first organized cheerleading in America took place at Princeton University in 1869, when a group of students organized to lead cheers at a football game against Rutgers University. Then during the 1880s, students at Princeton formed a pep squad specifically for cheering. The idea spread to other parts of the country when a Princeton graduate introduced organized cheerleading to the University of Minnesota.

A group of male cheerleaders from Columbia University pose with their team mascot in 1924. In the early years of the sport, most cheerleaders were men who used chants, cheers, and songs to energize both fans and the team.

The Birth of Animated Sign Stunts

In 1925, Lindley Bothwell, a male cheerleader at the University of Oregon, used flash cards, or signs, in a new way to increase audience participation. He passed out a thousand cards to spectators in the stands, and when the audience held up the cards, they formed the image of a beaver, the university's mascot. On Bothwell's signal, the crowd then waved the cards to make it appear as if the beaver was smashing the rival with its tail.

The stunt amazed the audience. It was so popular that other colleges began creating similar animated card stunts. The idea spread throughout the nation.

In 1889, the University of Minnesota's football team was having a bad run and had lost three games in a row. Students called for a plan that would inspire enthusiasm and motivate the team. In response, the pep club chose a group of male students to lead the cheering at the next game. Although they were called "yellers" at the time, these male students were the University of Minnesota's first cheerleaders. During the next football game, an elected yeller named Johnny Campbell used a megaphone to amplify his voice while leading cheers—a practice that would soon become standard in cheerleading. When the football team won its game, the cheerleaders were given some of the credit for their efforts in motivating the fans and the players.

Although cheerleading quickly became an organized activity, twenty-five years passed before it began to look anything like modern cheerleading. Today, most cheerleaders are female, and they perform complex routines that include jumps and stunts. In the early days, most cheerleaders were men, and they did not perform athletic skills. Instead, they used only their voices to get crowds excited during sporting events. They shouted, yelled, and sang to energize crowds at football, basketball, and rugby games.

By 1923, however, cheerleading began to evolve into a different kind of activity that more closely resembled modern cheerleading.

New Cheerleaders and New Cheers

Over the next several decades, the composition of cheerleading teams, the props they used, and the moves they made while cheering began to change. In 1923, women began to get involved in cheerleading. That year, the first female cheerleaders cheered at the University of Minnesota. Unlike modern cheerleaders, who typically wear short skirts and sleeveless vests, the original female cheerleaders wore long wool skirts and big, bulky sweaters with shirts underneath. In the 1930s, cheerleaders began to use props to help them motivate crowds, such as pom-poms. Created by inventor

High school cheerleaders wear sweaters and long skirts and hold crepe-paper pom-poms while performing at a football game in 1947.

Jim Hazzlewood, pom-poms were originally made of colored strips of crepe paper. Cheerleaders held one in each hand and waved them around to create an exciting visual in addition to their cheers.

For years, cheerleading continued as an activity dominated by men with some women participants, but during the 1940s that changed. When the United States entered World War II in 1941, many American men left college to enlist in the military and fight in the war. College activities, like cheerleading, were left to the female students who were still on campus. Suddenly, there were more female cheerleaders than male cheerleaders. Even after the war ended in 1945 and the men returned to college, female students decided to keep their positions and were more active in cheerleading squads than their male peers.

Herkimer and Modern Cheerleading

During the 1940s, cheerleading continued to evolve and became popular in both high school and college sporting events. A cheerleading innovator soon emerged on the scene who would change the face of cheerleading forever. Lawrence "Herkie" Herkimer, a cheerleader at Southern Methodist University in Texas who had also been a cheerleader in high school, invented a new cheerleading move—a jump called the Herkie. To perform this move, cheerleaders jumped straight up in the air and extended one leg out to the side. The other leg was bent at the knee, brought back behind the body. At the same time, one arm went straight up and the opposite hand was placed on the hip. The Herkie would become a signature cheerleading move. Herkimer, however, did not invent the jump on purpose. "It was just a poor split jump. I don't like to tell people that," [2] Herkimer admitted to the *New York Times* in 2009.

In 1948, after he had graduated from college, Herkimer was asked to hold a cheerleading camp at a Texas college to introduce cheerleading to interested students. That first year,

52 girls and 1 boy attended the clinic. The following year, Herkimer decided to hold another cheerleading camp. This time, 350 students attended, signaling a growing interest in the sporting activity.

Herkimer built on his success, and in 1953 he started the Cheerleading Supply Company, which sold uniforms and later manufactured pom-poms, which he called pom pons. In 1961, he went on to found the National Cheerleaders Association (NCA), which created cheer camps. The NCA soon employed fifteen hundred instructors each summer and taught tens of thousands of cheerleaders. According to *New York Times* writer John Branch, Herkimer was in the right place at the right time to help create modern cheerleading and elevate the sport to a new level. Branch writes,

> Herkimer basically invented [cheerleaders], the modern version, at least, then spawned generations more, until millions had attended his camps, wore his pleated skirts and clingy sweaters and bought his patented pompoms. They learned cheers that echoed from the crannies of the American landscape. They filled hot gyms and cool Friday nights with rhythmic soundtracks and ever-flouncing bursts of choreographed color.[3]

Thanks in large part to Herkimer and the NCA, cheerleading became a staple of American sporting events and a beloved national pastime.

The Addition of Advanced Movements

By the 1960s, nearly every high school and grade school in America had a cheerleading program. In 1974 another cheerleading organization was formed to advance the popular activity. Jeff Webb, who had worked for the NCA, founded the Universal Cheerleaders Association (UCA) with the goal of introducing more advanced movements into cheerleading. The organization also sought to create a set of skills specific to cheerleading.

Under the UCA's leadership, partner stunts (in which cheerleaders work in pairs) and pyramids (stunts in which several cheerleaders take part) became an integral part of cheerleading. The UCA also brought music to cheerleading, which led to the development of modern cheerleading routines, which

High school cheerleaders form a pyramid, one of several types of stunts that became an integral part of the sport beginning in the 1970s.

often incorporate popular music and dancelike moves. The UCA held training camps to spread the news of this new style of cheerleading.

Soon, so many coaches and cheerleaders across the country wanted to see what was happening in cheerleading that it became difficult to promote the activity through training camps alone. Webb decided it was time to televise the new developments. A new sports television network, called Entertainment Sports Programming Network, or ESPN, seemed like the perfect vehicle for national exposure. In 1982, the UCA's first Cheerleading National Championship was held, featuring cheerleading as a competitive, rather than a sideline, event. The championship was featured on ESPN, which helped to increase cheerleading's international exposure.

Cheerleading Goes International

From that point on, cheerleading was a regularly featured event on television. In the United States, cheerleading quickly became so popular that schools could not handle the demand. There was not enough room on existing squads for all the cheerleaders who wanted to be involved. By the 1990s, many nonschool-based programs, called All Star programs, were also available to cheerleaders. All Star cheerleading gave cheerleaders the chance to focus on training and competing rather than cheering for specific teams.

Cheerleaders in Japan perform during the opening ceremony of an athletic competition in 2007. Since the 1990s, the sport has become popular worldwide.

Cheerleading Joins the NFL

Cheerleading went professional when two female fans of the Baltimore Colts, a professional football team, organized a cheerleading squad for the team in 1954. There were ten women on the squad, the first of its kind to perform in the National Football League (NFL). They wore white boots, blue and gray skirts, crew-neck sweaters, and blue scarves. They even had a mascot, a real horse.

The Colts gave each cheerleader two tickets to each game. When the Colts traveled, the team paid the cheerleaders' expenses. But the cheerleaders bought their own clothing and made their own pom-poms. Their dedication was especially apparent on cold days, when they lined their boots with plastic bags to help keep their feet dry and kept on cheering for their team.

Cheerleading took off internationally during this time as well. In the two decades following the first national championship, the UCA introduced cheerleading all over the world through training camps, performances, and parades. Cheerleading became popular in many other countries, including Japan, England, Austria, France, Ireland, Chile, Costa Rica, Mexico, Canada, and Australia.

In 2003, the United States All Star Federation (USASF) and the International All Star Federation (IASF) were formed to support international cheerleading. The following year, the first World Cheerleading Championships were held. Similar to the National Cheerleading Championships but on a larger scale, this international competition went on to become an annual event.

Cheerleading as a Sport

Modern cheerleading is entertaining, exciting, athletic, and competitive, but there is still debate among some groups over whether cheerleading is truly a sport. In 2010, a federal judge ruled that a women's cheerleading squad at Quinnipiac College in Connecticut did not qualify as an official college sports team. Because the college receives federal funds, it is required to offer equal athletic opportunities for both men and women. This ruling meant that cheerleading was not eligible as a women's sports team at the college and, therefore, could not be funded with federal funds.

According to the judge, cheerleading was not a sport because it was "too underdeveloped and disorganized."[4] In an article for Fox News, journalist Diane Macedo explains that according to national regulations, "a sport must have coaches, practices, and competitions during a defined season. It must also have a governing organization, and its primary goal must be to compete, not just support other teams. But cheerleading advocates say their activity meets those requirements and more."[5] The ruling in the Quinnipiac College case could have a nationwide effect. Based on this decision, some colleges may decide to cut cheerleading programs if they are unable to fund the program without help from federal funds.

Cheerleaders from the University of Kentucky perform a flip during a basketball game. Advocates are working to have the NCAA recognize competitive cheer and cheerleader-style acrobatics and tumbling as an official sport.

Some cheerleading advocates have suggested creating a new name for competitive cheerleading, to set it apart from sideline cheerleading. USA Cheer, a governing body for cheerleading organizations, wants to create a sport called "stunt." The National Collegiate Athletics and Tumbling Association, a group of six competing universities, supports "team acrobatics and tumbling" as a cheerleading-style sport. Both groups have asked the National Collegiate Athletic Association (NCAA) to recognize competitive cheerleading as a sport. Bill Seely, executive director with USA Cheer, explains his organization's position: "We're trying to provide schools with a format that will work at the collegiate level.... One of our priorities is to make sure that it does not come at the expense of traditional cheerleading."[6]

As the debate heats up, many cheerleading advocates want to see cheerleading officially recognized as a sport, but like Seely, they often also want to preserve traditional sideline cheerleading and the qualities that motivational cheerleading represents. Webb explains,

> We support any effort that promotes cheerleading or that creates opportunities for women and girls. At the same time, we want to make sure that any sport designation does not take away the traditional role of cheerleading and that we preserve the very qualities that make cheerleading such an appealing activity for young people. I'm thinking of leadership, ambassadorship, service in the community: these are the character traits that cheerleading has always fostered.[7]

In the past, there was a great deal of concern that calling cheerleading a sport would trivialize female students' athletic abilities and would potentially restrict their access to other sports. Thomas writes,

> [Women] feared that calling it a sport sent the wrong message to women—endorsing an embarrassing holdover from a time when girls in tight-fitting outfits were expected to do little more than yell support for boys.

Those women were also skeptical of high schools and universities that counted female cheerleaders as athletes as a way to evade their obligation to provide opportunities for women in more traditional sports, like softball and soccer.[8]

Some observers feared that if cheerleading were labeled a sport, colleges and universities would use it to comply with Title IX of the Educational Amendments Act of 1972, which prohibits sex discrimination in schools. There have been high schools and colleges that called traditional sideline cheerleading a sport to prove they offered opportunities for women. However, sideline cheerleading did not offer athletic opportunities equal to other sports, including competitive cheerleading.

Today, the debate goes on, but one thing is clear. Whether or not it is officially designated as a sport, cheerleading requires strength, stamina, skill, and talent. It requires the same qualities that any athlete needs to exhibit while performing in his or her sport.

CHAPTER **2**

Chants and Cheers

Historically, cheerleaders have been known and appreciated for their ability to motivate crowds and teams through their vocalizations. Just like yellers did years ago, modern cheerleaders energize crowds by using their vocal skills and developing vocal techniques to boost their cheering power. Effective vocalizations are an essential aspect of both sideline and competitive cheerleading. "Cheering and chanting are the skills [used] most when performing," according to writer Sara Ipatenco. "The most effective cheerleaders have strong voices that carry across the court or the field so the players and crowd can easily hear what they are saying. It is essential that [they] cheer in [their] loudest voice and that [they] emphasize [their] words and really punch the sounds out."[9]

Several scientific principles lie behind the efforts cheerleaders make to improve their cheering. Cheerleaders produce the sounds they make when cheering and chanting through sound production steps that include respiration, phonation, articulation, and amplification.

Vocalization

To understand how cheering and chanting work on a scientific level, it is important to understand the difference between these two styles of vocalization. While both are used to capture a crowd's attention, cheers tend to be longer

Growing Up Cheerleading

When young male cheerleaders reach puberty, they may notice their voices cracking and breaking during cheers and chants. This occurs because their vocal folds and larynx are growing. Throughout childhood, a boy's vocal folds grow about 0.04 inches (0.10cm) in length each year. According to the website KidsHealth,

> before a boy reaches puberty, his larynx is pretty small and his vocal cords are kind of small and thin. That's why his voice is higher than an adult's. But as he goes through puberty, the larynx gets bigger and the vocal cords lengthen and thicken, so his voice gets deeper. Along with the larynx, the vocal cords grow significantly longer and become thicker. In addition, the facial bones begin to grow. Cavities in the sinuses, the nose, and the back of the throat grow bigger, creating more space in the face in which to give the voice more room to resonate.

The changes in a boy's voice only lasts a few months, so male cheerleaders can soon cheer and chant again without worrying that their voices will squeak.

"Your Changing Voice." KidsHealth. http://kidshealth.org/kid/grow/boy/changing_voice.html.

than chants. They also have a clear beginning and an end. Cheers are usually performed at sporting events during halftime, between quarters, or during time-outs. They include motions and encourage crowd participation in specific ways. "Cheers have more motions than claps, typically one motion per word," according to writer Jami Kastner. "Frequently, tumbling, stunting and jumping will be incorporated into a cheer. Often a cheer will include signs to encourage the crowd to yell along at certain points, and some squads incorporate poms [pom-poms] into their cheers as well."[10] This combination of choreographed movements and audience involvement is standard in any cheerleading routine.

Chants, however, tend to be shorter than cheers, and they repeat over and over without a clear ending. Kastner explains, "Chants are performed on the sidelines of a game, during the game. Chants have fewer motions and more claps, sometimes only having one motion at the end of the chant. The crowd should chant along with the

Cheerleaders from the University of Dayton hold cards spelling their team mascot's name while performing a cheer at a basketball game.

cheerleaders."[11] Chants are an essential element of sideline cheerleading, and cheerleading squads typically have a number of memorized chants that correspond with what is happening on the court or field—whether their team is playing offense or defense and whether their team is doing well or poorly. Cheerleading squads also develop crowd participation chants with a call-and-response format, with cheerleaders shouting out the first line and the crowd responding with an established response.

In order for cheerleading to effectively excite a crowd, cheerleaders need to amplify their voices to exceed the volume of the crowd and their surrounding conditions. If people in the crowd cannot understand what the cheerleaders are saying, they will not be motivated to get involved and respond. In order to be effective, cheers and chants have to be entertaining, easy to understand, and loud enough to command attention in a noisy environment. The first step to achieving this combination is proper breathing. Cheerleaders may not consciously focus on their breathing while they are cheering, but proper breathing helps them employ the specific techniques necessary for powerful vocalizations.

Breathing and the Respiratory System

The respiratory system is the system of organs in the body that controls breathing. It includes the nose, throat, larynx, trachea (windpipe), lungs, bronchi, and diaphragm. Humans

VOCAL FOLDS AND THE RESPIRATORY SYSTEM

The human respiratory system is made up of the nasal cavity, throat (pharynx), voice box (larynx), trachea, bronchi, lungs, and diaphragm. Vocal folds found in the voice box are manipulated by being brought closer together or farther apart to create vocalizations in a high or low pitch.

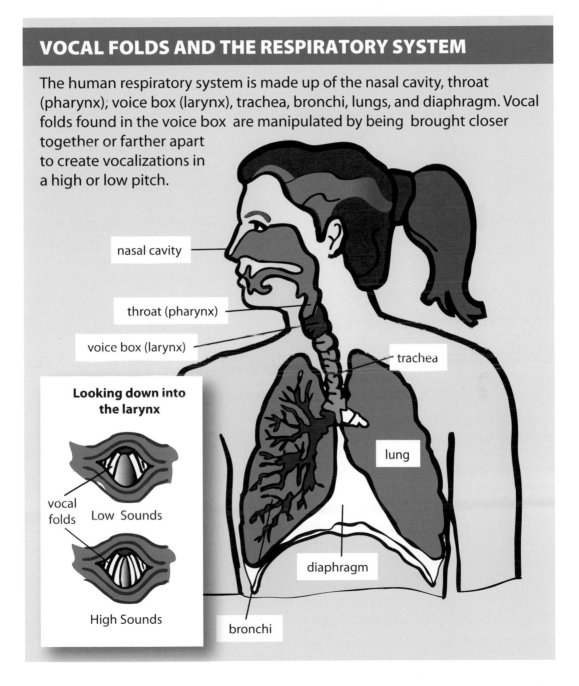

nasal cavity

throat (pharynx)

voice box (larynx)

trachea

lung

diaphragm

bronchi

Looking down into the larynx

vocal folds

Low Sounds

High Sounds

bring oxygen into their bodies by inhaling through the mouth or nose. The oxygen travels down the trachea to the bronchi, before moving into the lungs. In the lungs, the oxygen enters the red blood cells, which carry it throughout the body. Underneath the lungs, a dome-shaped muscle called the diaphragm contracts when humans inhale. This creates more space for the lungs to fill with oxygen. Humans exhale as carbon dioxide is forced out of their lungs when the diaphragm expands. Carbon dioxide, a waste gas, leaves the body through the mouth or nose. When it leaves the body through the mouth, it travels over the larynx.

The respiratory system plays a major role in cheering because cheerleaders regulate tone and pitch and amplify their voices when they exhale. They do this through a process called phonation. Cheerleaders also produce recognizable vocal sounds, such as language, by controlling their exhalation. This process is called articulation.

Phonation and Articulation

The creation of vocal sounds happens when carbon dioxide passes over the larynx, also called the voice box, through a process called phonation. This involves manipulation of the larynx as carbon dioxide moves over it, to adjust the voice's pitch and loudness. When carbon dioxide moves over the vocal folds in the larynx, the vocal folds vibrate, resulting in sound waves. According to the Voice Academy, a website maintained by the University of Iowa, "the faster your vocal folds vibrate, the higher the pitch of your voice. That is not due to the speed of respiration, but rather to the voluntary shaping of your vocal folds. Long, thin folds ripple quickly (high pitch). Shorter, bulkier vocal folds, then, produce lower pitches."[12] The volume of a vocalization, meanwhile, can be adjusted by manipulating the vocal folds and carbon dioxide pressure delivered by the lungs.

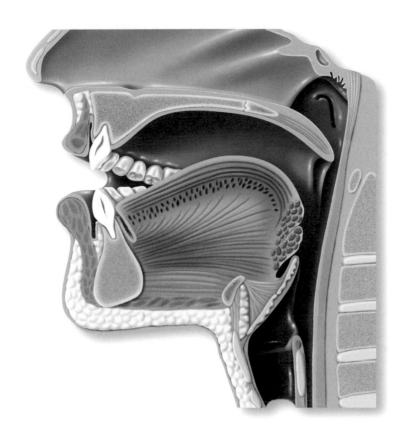

An illustration of the lower face shows the position of various parts of the mouth and throat, including the lips, teeth, tongue, uvula, palate, pharynx, and larynx, when a person pronounces the vowel sound "a." The position of these various parts changes to make the sounds of other letters.

Phonation creates vocal sounds, and these sounds are then shaped into language, and even familiar yells and whoops, through the process of articulation, which creates recognizable vocalizations and language. This process involves nineteen parts of the body between the lips and the vocal folds. These parts include the lips, teeth, palate, tongue, jaw, nasal cavity, and uvula, and each plays a role in creating specific sounds. The Voice Academy offers the following example: "We begin with a forceful puff of air [carbon dioxide] and use the upper and lower lips to make the sounds [p], [b] and [m]. Upper teeth and lower lip produce [f] and [v]. The backs of our tongues and the soft palates work together to produce [k] and [g]. For some sounds [h], all we do is open everything up and allow the sound to travel out the mouth."[13]

Cheerleaders can perform well without knowing exactly how phonation and articulation work to produce sound. But whether they realize it or not, they make special efforts to use these scientific processes to their advantage. Cheerleaders amplify their voices by creating pressure in their lungs. They take deep breaths that expand the diaphragm to push carbon dioxide and sound out forcefully. They also enunciate their words by using their mouth, teeth, tongue, and other structures to pronounce consonants clearly. They know that making these efforts will make their cheers and chants more powerful.

Pumping Up the Volume

One way to make cheers and chants more powerful is by making them louder. After all, they have to be heard to be effective. When cheerleaders amplify the volume of their voices, however, they do not just shout or scream over the noise of the crowd. When humans scream or shout, their vocal cords vibrate faster, creating high-pitched sounds. Cheerleaders could try to shout or scream at a higher volume than the crowd, but high-pitched voices do not sound commanding or even pleasant at a loud volume.

Instead, cheerleaders lower their pitch to amplify their voices. They do this by shaping their vocal folds so they are short and close together. When the folds are in this shape, more pressure is required to force carbon dioxide through them to create sounds. Cheerleaders create this pressure by breathing deeply to fill the lungs with oxygen and by relaxing the diaphragm when they exhale.

Low-pitched voices sound more commanding and carry farther than high-pitched voices. This is because they have longer wavelengths, which have more energy than shorter wavelengths and will travel longer and farther. Sound travels through the air as sound waves. A wavelength is the distance between the crests, or tops, of each individual wave. As these sound waves move, they vibrate the air particles in their path.

When the sound waves produced by the cheerleaders' chants and cheers reach a spectator in the crowd, the

HEARING CHEERS AND CHANTS

When sound waves created by a chant or cheer hit a listener's ear, they are funneled into the ear canal by the pinna, where they hit the eardrum and create vibrations that transfer into the bones in the middle ear and the structures of the inner ear. Stimulation of the auditory nerve sends signals to the brain, which then interprets auditory information.

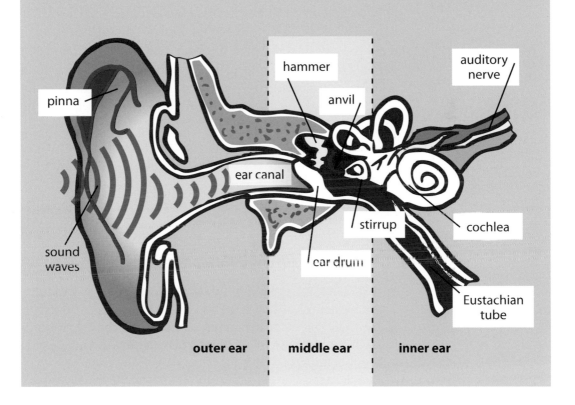

pinna

sound waves

ear canal

hammer

anvil

stirrup

ear drum

auditory nerve

cochlea

Eustachian tube

outer ear | **middle ear** | **inner ear**

sound waves and the vibrations they cause begin a journey into each ear through the ear canal where they cause vibrations in the eardrum. Structural elements in the middle ear, by the eardrum, pick up the vibrations and carry them to the cochlea in the inner ear. Within the inner ear, a structure known as the organ of Corti contains auditory sensory nerves that then carry the vibration information to the brain.

At that point, it is the brain's job to interpret the information being transmitted, such as a cheer or chant. This is called auditory processing. When people can clearly hear and understand what cheerleaders are cheering and chanting, they have the best chance of being able to interpret the information they hear correctly. They may listen and be inspired and excited. Or, they might join in by answering back or chanting along with the cheerleaders.

Vocal Training

Sporting events that have cheerleaders—like football and basketball games—can often last for hours. Cheerleaders must have the physical stamina to cheer and chant for an entire game. They also have to make sure their voices stay strong and in control while they perform movements to go along with their vocalizations. Cheerleaders must train for the endurance they need. Writer Cristina Lianchic, explains,

Since you will be out there cheering for several hours, you are going to need to have the physical capacity to

Vocal Coaches

Vocal coaches teach people how to sing and speak more effectively. They can also teach cheerleaders how to use their voices for maximum effect. Many vocal coaches teach clients how to maximize their breathing and use their breath to support their voice. This is especially important for cheerleaders, who perform stunts and dances while they are cheering and chanting.

Specific vocal exercises and techniques can help cheerleaders project their voices and produce sounds that resonate. They can also help cheerleaders prevent damage to their vocal folds. Cheerleader's voice syndrome is a condition in which the vocal cords rub together forcefully, creating a shrill sounding voice. Vocal coaches can help cheerleaders avoid developing cheerleader's voice syndrome and other side effects from overuse or improper use.

keep going the whole time. So you need to be sure to do some endurance training frequently … you've got to teach your body to be able to speak even while you are working out. Trust me: if you train your body to breathe, when it comes time to perform, you will continue breathing. And speaking. And cheering![14]

Cheerleaders must train to keep their voices loud and strong during long games.

Cheerleaders train for vocal endurance with specific exercises. For example, some exercises strengthen the diaphragm. Cheerleaders lie on their backs, bend their knees, and put one hand on the abdomen and one on the chest. They breathe in pushing the abdomen out and breathe out pulling the abdomen in. The chest remains still.

Another way cheerleaders prepare for lengthy performances is by doing special warm-up exercises beforehand. While warm-up exercises have not been scientifically proven to be effective, many professionals believe that they prepare the voice for excessive use and help prevent injury. The Voice and Swallowing Institute of New York, for example, recommends vocal warm-ups for professional voice users, such as cheerleaders:

The warm ups may increase blood flow to muscles and other tissues, thin out thick secretions, and decrease use of excessive muscular tension … we believe that warm ups improve the performance of the individual muscles of the thorax (chest), larynx and upper vocal tract (throat, mouth), as well as the coordination between the subsystems of voice production, namely the lungs, larynx, and upper airway articulators.[15]

There are many different kinds of vocal warm-up exercises cheerleaders can do. During a yawn-sigh exercise, cheerleaders will first yawn while inhaling. Next, they exhale slowly, keeping the jaw, head, and shoulders relaxed. While they exhale, they make a sound, varying the pitch of the sound for five seconds. In another warm-up exercise, cheerleaders will breathe deeply then make a "huh!" sound on the exhale. The sound comes from contracting the abdominal muscles while keeping the structures of the upper airway (larynx and throat) open and relaxed.

Some cheerleaders also do warm downs, or cooldowns, after a performance. They have not been scientifically proven to be effective either, but they may be physiologically beneficial. According to the Voice and Swallowing Institute, warm downs

[are] not as commonly used as warm ups [and] some performers find it helpful to perform a short routine of gentle vocalizing, such as relaxed humming, massage of the neck, throat, and lower face, easily "cooing" the /u/ vowel (as in coo). It may be that warm downs help release some of [the] excessive muscle tension that may accumulate during rehearsal or performance, especially in vocally demanding roles.[16]

Vocal specialists can help cheerleaders plan the most beneficial training programs for vocal endurance. They can also help plan warm-up and cooldown programs to keep cheerleaders' voices healthy. In addition, vocal specialists can help if cheerleaders strain or damage their vocal cords from too much cheering. Vocal specialists include laryngologists, who are surgeons who treat voice, breathing, and swallowing disorders, and speech-language pathologists, who treat disorders in speech, language, cognitive communication, voice, swallowing, and fluency.

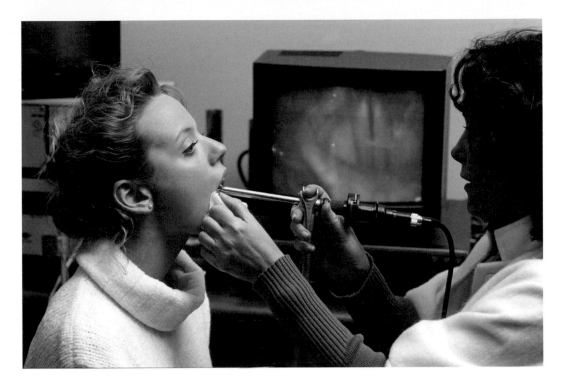

Most vocal specialists agree that it is critical that cheerleaders pay attention to their vocal health before, during, and after performances. The Lions Voice Clinic of Minneapolis, Minnesota, for example, advocates good vocal hygiene for all professional voice users, including cheerleaders. Vocal hygiene is the practice of caring for the human voice and maintaining a healthy vocal system. The voice clinic advises that individuals should be mindful of their vocal health and become familiar with their own voice: "The more you know about your voice and how it works, the safer you are. The more you understand the individual characteristics of your OWN voice, the safer you are."[17] Proper vocal care for chants and cheers is just one element of cheerleading, but mastering vocal techniques and developing vocal strength is essential as cheerleaders move into more complicated routines.

A vocal specialist performs a laryngoscopy to examine a young woman's throat, larynx, and vocal cords. Such specialists can advise cheerleaders on techniques for keeping their voices healthy.

CHAPTER 3

Dance Moves

Today's cheerleaders do much more than cheer and chant. They use their entire bodies to create exciting performances, often incorporating dance steps into their routines. These steps are also often choreographed to music.

Because cheerleading so often includes dance moves, cheerleaders are sometimes compared to dancers. As writer Chris Callaway explains on the website Livestrong.com, "cheerleading and dance share many similarities. Both require a great deal of athleticism, yet both have been questioned as to whether they are a sport. Both can involve choreographed movements set to music…. There are hundreds of types of dance…. Cheerleading borrows moves and techniques from most … types of dance."[18]

There is some debate as to whether cheerleaders who dance should be considered dancers. Regardless of how they are classified, cheerleaders, like dancers, need flexibility, energy, and control to perform their moves precisely. It all begins with learning how to execute these moves.

Dance Steps and Motor Learning

Cheerleaders learn to execute dance moves through the complex process of motor learning, which has four phases—observation, replication, feedback, and repetition. During the observation phase, cheerleaders watch others

BRAIN STRUCTURES AND MOTOR LEARNING

Cheerleaders learn to perform new dance moves through motor learning. The four phases of motor learning—observation, replication, feedback, and repetition—involve the complex function of several parts of the brain.

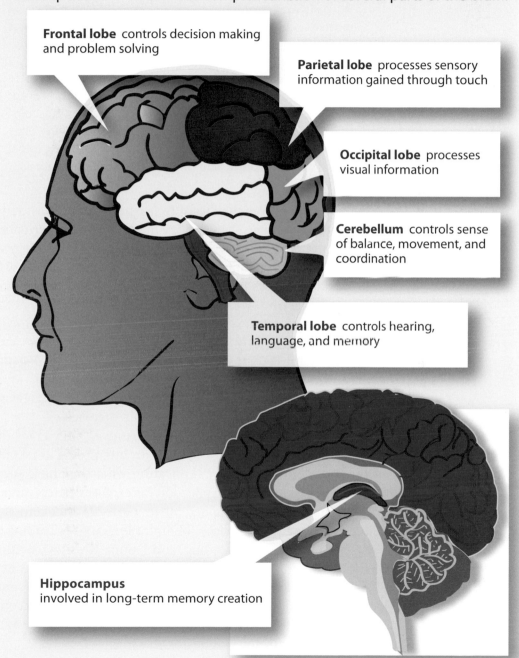

Frontal lobe controls decision making and problem solving

Parietal lobe processes sensory information gained through touch

Occipital lobe processes visual information

Cerebellum controls sense of balance, movement, and coordination

Temporal lobe controls hearing, language, and memory

Hippocampus involved in long-term memory creation

Dance Physiotherapists

Physiotherapists, also called physical therapists, are therapists who treat injuries and disorders through physical means, such as exercise or massage. Dance physiotherapists are simply physiotherapists who specialize in treating dancers. They can also treat gymnasts and cheerleaders.

Physiotherapists not only work with patients to help them recover from an injury, but they also help patients prevent injury. Dance physiotherapists focus on treating musculoskeletal conditions that limit dancers' ability to move. They help rehabilitate dancers through specialized exercises, spinal manipulation therapy, acupuncture, and other treatments.

perform the moves they want to learn. Coaches may demonstrate skills themselves, or they may ask more experienced squad members to perform skills while beginners observe them. Researchers have found that observing in this way helps cheerleaders and other athletes learn complex muscle movements. Andrew A.G. Mattar and Paul L. Gribble of the University of Western Ontario, Canada, studied this process and report, "When we observe the actions of others, we activate the same [brain] circuitry responsible for planning and executing our own actions. By observing another individual learning to move accurately in a novel mechanical environment, observers move more accurately themselves."[19]

After cheerleaders observe dance moves, they enter the replication phase of motor learning by attempting to execute the moves themselves by replicating what they have seen. While observing makes replication easier, cheerleaders cannot perform their choreographed moves perfectly after completing only the first two phases of motor learning. According to authors Virginia Wilmerding, and Donna Krasnow, writing for the International Association for Dance Medicine & Science, "it is likely that the first attempts would include some wobbling and adjusting, as the brain seeks strategies to accomplish this shift [dance move] in a smooth, coordinated way as demonstrated by the teacher [or coach]."[20]

During the replication phase, the feedback phase begins as cheerleaders receive feedback on their replication efforts from both external and internal sources. In addition to receiving verbal feedback from their coach, cheerleaders listen for cues from the music to tell them whether they are performing the right movements at the right time, and they feel their feet on the floor and make adjustments to their position for better balance. They may also practice in front of a mirror to get a visual image of their own performance.

Within their own bodies, cheerleaders also receive feedback from nerve fibers called proprioceptors. These fibers are located in bones, muscles, tendons, ligaments, joints, and skin. Proprioceptors deliver information about motion and body position to the central nervous system, which includes the brain and spinal cord. Proprioceptors also work with the vestibular system, which controls balance in the inner ear, as well as the visual system, or sight. The feedback cheerleaders get from their proprioceptors helps them keep their balance and move fluidly while transferring their body weight to execute dance moves.

Once cheerleaders can execute the dance moves properly, they move into the repetition phase of motor learning, which means they practice the dance moves over and over again. Wilmerding, and Krasnow explain,

With repetition, [the dance moves become] a part of the dancer's long-term memory. When the same or similar movements are required, the dancer must recall it mentally (referred to as covert recall) and transfer it to physical execution (referred to as overt recall). By the time the motor skill is imbedded in long-term memory, it is an image or concept of the task that is recalled at this level of execution, rather than a complicated series of details, multiple body parts, or individual muscle activation.... Once the appropriate neurological pattern is set up (i.e., the movement is being executed correctly and efficiently), repetition will ingrain the skill into the body, much the same way as walking on the neighbor's perfect yard will wear a path through it.[21]

Once cheerleaders have repeated a dance routine a number of times, it requires less concentration to complete, letting cheerleaders focus on other elements in the performance.

Warming Up for Dance

To learn and perform dance routines, cheerleaders need flexibility, energy, and strength. Dance routines are demanding, and cheerleaders perform specific exercises to gain the physical skills these routines require. Cheerleaders warm up for dancing with aerobic and stretching exercises. The process of warming up prepares the entire nervous system for physical activity. Without warming up, any athlete is at risk for injury or fatigue while performing.

Aerobic exercises, such as jumping rope, walking, or jogging, warm up the body by raising the heart rate and breathing rate. When the heart pumps faster, more blood flows

A cheerleader stretches her legs and back in order to warm up her muscles and improve her flexibility.

to muscles through the circulatory system, which includes the heart, lungs, and blood vessels. Increased blood flow warms and relaxes muscles. Blood also delivers oxygen and nutrients to muscles. When the breathing rate increases, more oxygen is delivered to muscles. This is important because when oxygen reaches the muscles, it breaks down carbohydrates, fats, and proteins to create adenosine triphosphate (ATP). Muscles use ATP for energy.

Stretching exercises have multiple benefits for cheerleaders when they are warming up. Stretching muscles stimulates synovial fluid production. Synovial fluid is a slippery liquid that lubricates joints, making movement easier. Stretching also helps distribute synovial fluid in the body, making it easier for cheerleaders to move and increase their flexibility. Cheerleaders increase their flexibility by stretching muscles and ligaments in two different ways. Static stretches, such as splits or back bends, are stationary. To perform static stretches, cheerleaders hold a position for thirty to sixty seconds without moving. Dynamic stretches involve movement. To perform dynamic stretches, cheerleaders may use the same positions used in static stretches, but they contract their muscles and stretch beyond their normal range of motion. Dynamic stretches lengthen muscle tissue and encourage the body to adapt to more difficult positions. This allows cheerleaders to move with more flexibility.

Building Endurance Through Exercise

After warming up with aerobic exercise or stretches, cheerleaders are ready for more strenuous activity, which often includes cardiovascular exercise, such as running or biking. This kind of exercise may not seem closely related to dance or dance technique, but it has an important function. It helps cheerleaders build stamina and endurance for their year-round athletic season and extensive dance routines.

Cheerleaders and Birds

In his research, Aniruddh D. Patel, a doctor in theoretical neurobiology at the Neurosciences Institute in San Diego, California, learned about a cockatoo named Snowball that seemed to be dancing in a popular YouTube video. Patel watched the video and wanted to learn more. He called the director of the bird shelter where Snowball lived and proposed an experiment. They videotaped Snowball moving to the beat of the same song as the song was slowed down and sped up. The bird seemed to have a sense of rhythm regardless of the speed of the song. The outcome led Patel to see a link between human brains and bird brains.

"What do humans have in common with parrots? Both species are vocal learners, with the ability to imitate sounds," Patel said in an interview. "We share that rare skill with parrots. In that one respect, our brains are more like those of parrots than chimpanzees."

Quoted in Claudia Dreifus, "Exploring Music's Hold on the Mind." *New York Times*, May 31, 2010. http://www.nytimes.com/2010/06/01/science/01conv.html?partner =rss&emc=rss.

Specifically, cardiovascular exercise develops slow-twitch muscles. Slow-twitch muscles contract slowly and allow cheerleaders to perform athletic skills for hours at a time when cheering at a game. They also help cheerleaders maintain stamina for competitive routines. "A competitive cheerleading routine is just 2½ minutes long, but cheerleaders must cheer, dance, jump, tumble and stunt the entire time," writes Jami Kastner for Livestrong.com. "In order to perform for 2 ½ minutes straight, competitive cheerleaders need endurance. Cardiovascular exercise is what will build endurance."[22]

Focusing on Legs and Feet

When cheerleaders dance, they use their arms for balance and emphasis, but their feet and legs do most of the work. "Strong legs are important in all aspects of cheerleading.

They help in building stunts and pyramids, they help in gymnastics, and they help in jumps,"[23] explains writer Julie Anne Sommers. In order to make sure their feet and legs have the strength for dancing, and especially for jumps in routines, cheerleaders do specific exercises to strengthen and condition their legs and feet.

Lunges and squats are good exercises for building muscle strength. Lunges begin in a standing position. Cheerleaders step one foot forward, then bend their back knee almost to the ground. They then push their bodies back into the standing position with the forward leg. Squats are performed by standing with the feet slightly more than shoulder-width apart. Cheerleaders then bend their knees to a ninety-degree angle, almost as if they are sitting in the air, and then straighten them again. "The main muscles that are worked during lunges are the quadriceps, but the calves, glutes and hamstrings are also engaged," according to writer Dan Harriman. "Squats engage the same muscle groups in addition to the lower back."[24]

Many cheerleaders also do calf raises, which are performed by rising onto the toes and back down again, while in a standing position. This specifically builds strength in the calf muscles, but according to writer Alexis Kragenbrink Jenkins, it also does more than that. "Though you might not realize or feel it, calf raises actually are effective in stretching and strengthening the muscles of your feet, your arch and even your Achilles tendon,"[25] she writes.

Cheerleaders can also perform exercises to condition their feet for strength and flexibility. Strength exercises include walking on the heels, walking on the toes, spreading the toes out and pulling them back in, and standing with feet flat on the ground then lifting one toe at a time. The American Orthopaedic Foot and Ankle Society recommends several additional exercises dancers can do to increase foot flexibility. They include toe exercises that involve raising, pointing, and curling the toes; golf ball rolls, in which dancers roll a golf ball under the ball of the foot; and towel curls, in which dancers curl their toes around a towel on the floor. Picking up marbles with the toes and walking in the sand are also recommended. "Whether you are a ballroom dancer, a ballerina, hip-hop or tap dancer … having strong feet is an important part of a dancer's physique," notes Jenkins. "Healthy, strong feet can improve technique, increase stamina, make your movements flow with more grace and precision and improve your height and stride when you jump or leap. Most importantly, properly exercising your feet muscles and tendons can help prevent falls, strains and sprains."[26]

When cheerleaders perform any of the above exercises, they do repetitions, repeating the exercise several times in what is called a set. After a set, they may rest briefly before repeating the exercise several more times in successive sets. The idea is to work specific muscles more than usual, so they will be stimulated to adapt to the greater demand and different kinds of movements. As writer Elizabeth Quinn explains,

> Adaptation refers to the body's ability to adjust to increased or decreased physical demands. It is also one way we learn to coordinate muscle movement and develop sports-specific skills, such as batting, swimming freestyle or shooting free throws. Repeatedly practicing a skill or activity makes it second-nature and easier to perform. Adaptation explains why beginning exercisers are often sore after starting a new routine, but after doing the same exercise for weeks and months they have little, if any, muscle soreness.[27]

Repetition of exercises and adaption to these muscle movements can help cheerleaders develop the skills and stamina needed to perform successful cheerleading routines.

Choreography and Synchronization

When cheerleaders dance, they do more than perform specific movements. They also perform these movements in a specified sequence. Dance routines are choreographed to music, and cheerleaders synchronize their moves, meaning the moves match the music and the movements of their squad mates.

Research suggests that synchronization is an ability that starts in the brain, using the same neural pathways cheerleaders use to listen and learn vocal language. Aniruddh D. Patel, a doctor in theoretical neurobiology at the Neurosciences Institute in San Diego, California, studied the relationship between music and language. He found that the brain functions in similar ways when processing music and language. Patel suggests that the ability to synchronize dance movements to music, much like language development, may develop in both the auditory and movement centers of the brain. He explains, "Since vocal learning creates links between the hearing and movement centers of the brain, I hypothesized that this is what you need to be able to move to the beat of music."[28]

Cheerleaders from the University of Colorado move in synch during a dance routine, which requires extensive interaction between the brain and muscles.

Many parts of the brain are engaged while cheerleaders perform their choreographed routines. As they dance, the moves they perform are planned in the brain's frontal lobe. Here, the premotor cortex and supplementary motor area communicate information, such as the body's physical position in space and the memory of specific movements. This information is given to the primary motor cortex, which delivers information through the spinal cord to the specific muscles that need to contract to create the movements. As the muscles work, they send information back to the brain. The cerebellum takes in the information, so cheerleaders can perfect their movements and balance. In an article for the journal *Scientific American*, Steven Brown and Lawrence M. Parsons explain, "The cerebellum receives input from the spinal cord and appears to act something like a metronome [an instrument that keeps rhythm for musicians by clicking], helping to synchronize dance steps to music."[29] These complex interactions between the brain and the body allow cheerleaders to perfect their choreographed routines.

Energizing Music

The cheers, chants, and dances of cheerleaders can energize and motivate a crowd, but the music used during a routine to can also cause physical responses in both the cheerleaders and the crowd. Multiple areas in the brain are stimulated while listening to music, triggering a variety of results. Patel explains, "People sometimes ask where in the brain music is processed and the answer is everywhere above the neck.... Music engages huge swathes of the brain—it's not just lighting up a spot in the auditory cortex."[30] Research has found that music can cause changes in brain waves, breathing rate,

A Georgia Tech cheerleader gives an energetic performance during a dance routine. Upbeat music has an effect on the brain that pumps up cheerleaders and fans alike.

blood pressure, and heart rate. The effects of music on the body are so significant, that therapists often use music to help patients suffering from illness.

One way that music therapy works is by triggering the release of dopamine, a neurotransmitter in the brain that creates good feelings. Similarly, when cheerleaders choose the music for their dance routines, they want songs that will make them and their audience feel good. They generally select familiar tunes with a fast beat, possibly not realizing there is a scientific reason that familiar songs are a good choice. According to journalist Carolyn Butler, "brain researchers have found that listening to your favorite melodies and harmonies can trigger the release of large amounts of dopamine, a chemical that sends 'feel good' signals to the rest of the body and plays a role in both motivation and addiction."[31]

While familiar songs make people feel good, fast songs can trigger the release of adrenaline. Adrenaline is a hormone released from the adrenal glands that causes physical changes, including an increased heart rate and breathing rate. In effect, adrenaline raises a person's energy level. When cheerleaders choose fast songs, they are increasing their chances of getting spectators excited by raising their energy levels. They are also raising their own energy levels, so they can create a more lively performance and prepare for complex routines.

CHAPTER **4**

Tumbling and Jumping

When cheerleaders incorporate tumbling and jumps into their routines, they are putting a number of physics principles into action. "Cheerleading is an athletic activity that is chock full of physics principles," writes Kindra Harvey, for Livestrong.com. "Whether cheerleaders are creating momentum, acceleration, rotation or demonstrating [sheer] force, they always seem to have [mathematician and physicist Sir Issac] Newton and his laws [of motion] surrounding their every move. Understanding the physics of cheerleading is beneficial for performance. This understanding can also provide you with the knowledge to prevent injury and awareness of your safety."[32] During routines, cheerleaders convert potential energy, or stored energy, into kinetic energy, the energy of motion. They also use momentum, the force of motion, to achieve more height and speed in their movements.

Tumbling

In cheerleading, the term *tumbling* is used to describe gymnastics moves that require rotation of the body. Tumbling includes basic moves, such as forward and backward rolls, as well as more advanced moves, such as cartwheels and handsprings. Learning the basics gives cheerleaders the chance to master elements required to perform each move, including

THE AXES OF ROTATION

All cheerleading movements are performed around three axes of rotation of the human body: the medial axis, the longitudinal axis, and the transverse axis.

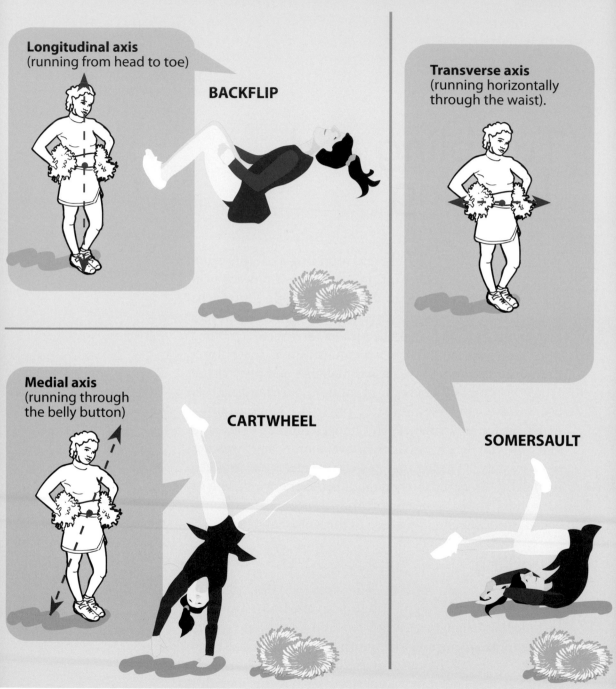

Longitudinal axis
(running from head to toe)

BACKFLIP

Transverse axis
(running horizontally through the waist).

Medial axis
(running through the belly button)

CARTWHEEL

SOMERSAULT

flexibility, coordination, balance, and muscle strength. All of these elements are used to perform advanced tumbling moves as well.

When cheerleaders perform tumbling, they rotate their body on one of three axes of movement. The transverse axis is an imaginary line running horizontally across the waist. Moves such as forward and backward rolls are performed on the transverse axis, as cheerleaders rotate around this imaginary line.

Some tumbling is performed on the longitudinal axis, an imaginary line running vertically from head to toe. A backward full, for instance, is a backward flip with one full twist in the longitudinal axis, performed from a standing position with the cheerleader's body straight.

Tumbling is also performed on the medial axis. This is an imaginary line running through the torso from back to front. Cheerleaders perform a cartwheel by standing with legs apart and arms stretched out to create an X shape. Holding this position, they tilt to the side so one hand touches the ground while one foot leaves the ground. They keep rotating over the medial axis so their second hand touches the ground while their second foot leaves the ground. As they continue to rotate, each of their feet returns to the ground until they are once again standing in an upright position.

When cheerleaders perform tumbling, they need good balance so they do not tip over or fall out of position. Cheerleaders have to maintain balance by making adjustments as their center of gravity shifts. The center of gravity is an imaginary point where weight is concentrated in the body, keeping the body in balance. In humans, this point is located somewhere in the torso. This point shifts when cheerleaders move and the weight of their arms and legs is redistributed away from, or close to, the trunk. They have to compensate for these shifts to maintain stability.

Muscle Memory

As cheerleaders become more advanced in tumbling, their muscles remember what they have learned. According to Adam Knight, an assistant professor of biomechanics at

Healthy Eating

Cheerleaders need a balanced diet that is high in carbohydrates and low in fat. During digestion, carbohydrates break down to create sugars, including glycogen, which is used by fast-twitch muscles. Simple carbohydrates, found in foods like fruit and milk products, break down very quickly for a burst of energy. Complex carbohydrates, found in foods like rice and grain products, provide more long-lasting energy because they break down more slowly.

Lean protein, found in foods like chicken and dairy products, helps cheerleaders replenish the energy they use to perform. The body breaks down proteins into amino acids that are used to rebuild muscle tissue. Protein also becomes an energy source when excess amino acids are metabolized into glycogen.

Mississippi State University, and Wayne Westcott, fitness research director at Quincy College in Massachusetts, muscle memory starts with proprioception. Cheerleaders' muscles, tendons, and joints give continuous feedback to the central nervous system through proprioceptors. That feedback creates new pathways, or memories, so repeated moves can be completed faster and eventually may become almost automatic.

There may be more to muscle memory, too, according to Norwegian scientists cited in an article for *Women's Health* magazine written by Selene Yeager. "Turns out, exercise also triggers long-term, possibly permanent, changes in your cells," she writes. "In a study of mice, researchers found that after just six days of simulated strength training, the mice generated new nuclei in their muscle cells. This is a big deal, since these nuclei contain the DNA blueprint necessary to make new muscle. And months after the mice stopped training, even though their muscles had shrunk, those newly formed nuclei were still hanging around, waiting to be reactivated by exercise."[33] This indicates that exercising and practicing their routines can make it easier for cheerleaders to perform and to form new muscle tissue.

Getting Airborne

There are many different styles of jumps that cheerleaders may incorporate into their routines. In the toe touch, cheerleaders jump into the air stretching their legs straight out to the sides and stretching their arms out to touch their toes. In the pike, cheerleaders jump up and put their legs straight out in front of them, with their arms reaching out in front as well. When performing the Herkie, cheerleaders straighten one leg out to the side and bend the other at the knee, with their arms straight out to the sides.

To perform any of these jumps, cheerleaders need to get airborne. This means overcoming gravity and friction to move vertically into the air. Gravity is the force that pulls the body down toward the earth. Friction is created when one surface moves against another, and it causes resistance to motion. It is created when cheerleaders push through air molecules to perform a jump.

Cheerleaders use potential energy, momentum, and kinetic energy to overcome gravity and friction in a vertical jump. Each vertical jump begins with the approach. As cheerleaders

A cheerleader performs a toe touch, which requires her to overcome gravity and friction to successfully execute the jump.

begin a jump, they swing their arms down and bend their knees. In doing this, they expend kinetic energy, or the energy of motion. From this position—with knees bent, prepared to jump—cheerleaders have potential energy, or stored energy. This potential energy is converted to kinetic energy when they swing their arms up and straighten their legs to jump. By swinging additional mass—their arms—in the direction they are moving, cheerleaders create momentum, a force that helps them overcome gravity. Momentum also helps cheerleaders overcome the friction created as their molecules push past air molecules to complete a jump.

Gaining Height

Gaining height is the second part of performing a jump. It is critical that cheerleaders achieve enough height to perform the jump properly before gravity brings them back to the ground. One way they achieve height is by creating momentum as they jump up.

Due to momentum, when cheerleaders jump up, they continue moving upward. This follows the First Law of Motion developed by Sir Isaac Newton, a mathematician and physicist in the late seventeenth and early eighteenth centuries. The First Law of Motion states that an object in motion will tend to stay in motion unless stopped by an outside force. This law is evident when cheerleaders jump and move up through they air. They keep moving up until they are stopped by gravity.

According to Newton's Second Law of Motion, the acceleration, or change in speed, of an object is related to the force acting upon it. In cheerleading, this means that more force is required to move cheerleaders with more body mass and less force is required to move cheerleaders with less body mass. Newton's Third Law of Motion states that for every action, there is an opposite and equal reaction. An example of this law is when cheerleaders return to the ground after a jump.

A cheerleader achieves height in a jump by creating momentum that will send her upward until she is stopped by gravity.

Body Position

Form is another essential component of a cheerleading jump. Cheerleaders have to create the correct body position in the air for the jump they have chosen to do. To accomplish this, cheerleaders put their proprioception to work while airborne, to determine where they are in space as they twist or turn. They also need to develop a sense of where they are in relation to the ground in order to land safely.

THE BACK TUCK

One common tumble in cheerleading is the back tuck. During this move, the cheerleader may pull in his or her arms and legs while performing the tumble. This decreases the body's radius—the distance from the body's center of gravity—and increases the body's rotational velocity, or speed through the movement. This will help the cheerleader make a complete rotation and land the tumble on both feet.

SPEED

Slow

Fast

Radiu

Center of gravity

Radius

Radius

Center of gravity

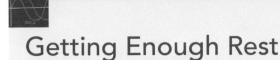

Getting Enough Rest

Cheerleaders need about nine to ten hours of sleep per night. Lack of sleep can affect athletic performance negatively by causing slower reaction times and slower cognitive functioning. Research indicates getting extra rest can actually improve athletic performance. According to writer Elizabeth Quinn,

> researchers speculate that deep sleep helps improve athletic performance because this is the time when growth hormone is released. Growth hormone stimulates muscle growth and repair, bone building and fat burning, and helps athletes recover. Studies show that sleep deprivation slows the release of growth hormone. Sleep is also necessary for learning a new skill, so this phase of sleep may be critical for some athletes.

Elizabeth Quinn. "Athletes and Sleep." About.com, June 16, 2009. http://sports-medicine.about.com/od/anatomyandphysiology/a/Athletes-Sleep.htm.

It takes practice to execute jumps correctly. And not all of that practice takes place in the air. As writer Jami Kastner explains, "the jumps, tumbling and stunting involved in cheerleading require a cheerleader to know many body positions. Cheerleaders must possess good body awareness to master these positions and use proper form to get the positions just right. Whether jumping, tumbling, or stunting, [cheerleaders should] master all body positions on the ground prior to attempting them in the air."[34] Form is essential to a good jump, but for cheerleaders to perform a successful and safe routine they must also perfect their landing.

A Controlled Landing

The last part of a jump is the landing. To land safely after a jump, cheerleaders must absorb the forces that are created as they hit the ground: contact force and impact force. Contact

Cheerleaders performing in a competition prepare to land after executing a jump. Their bent knees, hips, and ankles will allow their bodies to absorb the forces of impact from their landing.

force is created when two objects come together, such as when a cheerleader's feet touch the ground. Impact force is how hard the cheerleader lands. Impact force is calculated based on the mass of a cheerleader's body, the speed at which he or she is falling, and how that speed is accelerating due to the force of gravity.

Biomechanics, the science of how forces work on the body, comes into play as cheerleaders land and must handle contact and impact forces. When landing, cheerleaders need to position their bodies in specific ways to absorb contact and impact forces. When they land, they put their weight on the balls of their feet first. Then, they distribute that weight onto their heels by bending at the knees, hips, and ankles and rolling their feet onto the ground, from the balls to the heels. In addition, they distribute their weight evenly on each side of their body, so they will remain balanced and not fall over once they have landed. Cheerleaders also use cushioned mats on the ground to help absorb landing forces.

Training and Conditioning

Cheerleaders need muscle strength and flexibility for tumbling and jumping. For these particular skills they need to develop fast-twitch muscles. Cheerleaders use fast-twitch muscles to make quick, explosive movements. Fast-twitch muscles do not have the stamina of slow-twitch muscle fibers, which can expand and contract repeatedly for longer periods of time because they use energy all at once to

Exercises such as crunches that work the abdominal, oblique, and back muscles will increase a cheerleader's core strength and improve the ability to tumble and jump.

Go, Team!

Olympic gymnast Shawn Johnson is helping to promote a new cheerleading safety campaign. She partnered with Top Gun, an All Star program, and GK Elite, a sportswear company, to speak out on a video that brings attention to the issue.

contract quickly and forcefully. They do provide a combination of force and power, however.

To develop fast-twitch muscles, cheerleaders may do plyometrics, exercises that stretch muscles then contract them forcefully, such as vertical jumps. Plyometrics have three stages: the pre-stretch stage, the stretching stage, and the contracting stage. To perform a vertical jump, cheerleaders bend their legs at the hips, knees, and ankles to contract their muscles, lower their center of gravity, and create potential energy. When they jump up forcefully, they stretch the muscles, overloading them. As a result, the body develops more fast-twitch muscles in that area over time to handle the added work, so cheerleaders have more strength, speed, and power in their movements.

Cheerleaders also need core strength to perform tumbling and jumps. The core is made up of the abdominals, the obliques, and the lower back. Sports columnist Graig White explains why the core is so important to strong cheerleading:

> Your core muscles work to enable you to maintain good posture and to stabilize your upper body or trunk. Having a strong core means tumbling runs can be executed with much less effort and for greater distances, tops [cheerleaders at the top of pyramids] can maintain better balance, and cheerleading bases [cheerleaders at the bottom of pyramids] can hold tops more easily.... Core stability is what helps your muscles exert greater power. The core helps transfer energy through the body. For example, when executing a jump, the energy must pass through the core to elevate the body; without a good strong core, that energy will not be used as efficiently as it could be. Training the stabilizing muscles to hold the torso steady while introducing resistance from the arms, legs, and even gravity, is important.[35]

Exercises for strengthening the core include crunches, curl ups, side bends, Supermans and good mornings, which all focus on strengthening abdominal muscles and reinforcing proper posture. To perform a Superman, cheerleaders lie face down on the floor with their arms extended forward. They raise their right arm and left leg and hold, then repeat on the other side. Cheerleaders perform Good Mornings by standing with their feet shoulder width apart, knees bent and shoulders over their hips. They then put their hands on their hips and bend forward at the waist. Keeping their back and neck straight, they bend until their upper body is parallel with the floor. They lift back up to the starting position and repeat the movement.

When cheerleaders train and condition for even the most basic tumbling and jumps, they gain experience, flexibility, and muscle strength. This makes it possible for them to attempt, practice, and master more advanced cheerleading moves, including stunts and pyramids.

CHAPTER **5**

Stunts and Pyramids

S tunts and pyramids can be the most challenging moves that cheerleaders perform. Impressive stunts and pyramids send cheerleaders high into the air and include moves that appear dangerous, even impossible. As explained on Cheer Place, a cheerleading information resource website,

> great stunts [are] what many cheerleading squads strive for. Stunts add flair to a cheerleading routine. Stunts can be used to help lead the crowd with a cheer. They can also be used during music segments to build excitement or difficulty in a competition routine. What everyone must remember though, is [stunts] can be the most dangerous. If not taking the proper care while stunting, someone may get seriously hurt.[36]

Strength, agility, flexibility, coordination, and balance make these moves possible and safe to perform. The moves also take practice and experience.

Performing Stunts and Pyramids

In stunts and pyramids, cheerleaders work together to create performances with height and movement. Some cheerleaders are in support positions, holding up other cheerleaders.

Those in support positions are called the bases. The cheerleaders on top of the bases are called tops, or flyers.

Stunts are performed when one or more cheerleaders are bases and one or more cheerleaders are tops. Cheerleaders often learn how to do stunts and pyramids by first learning partner stunts, which have just one base and one top. For example, in the stunt called the chair, the base holds the top above his or her head, supporting the top at the ankle and thigh. The top extends one leg down and bends the other at the knee to assume a sitting position. Both arms are up in the air.

Cheerleaders from Boston University practice a complex pyramid formation using bases, flyers, and spotters.

After learning partner stunts, cheerleaders advance to basic stunts that include more bases and/or tops. The thigh stand, for example, requires two bases and one top. The two bases, facing each other, each perform a lunge, one with the right leg and one with the left leg. They bend their legs at the knee so their knees almost touch. The top puts his or her hands on the bases' shoulders and steps up onto the bases' thighs. The bases hold the top at the knees and feet. The top then stands, locks his or her knees, and raises his or her arms.

Building on the skills it takes to perform partner and basic stunts, cheerleaders work up to pyramids, which connect several stunts. In the handstand pyramid, for example, three separate stunts come together. In the center, bases hold up a top who stands with legs straight and arms extended upward. On the right and left of this stunt, bases hold up tops who are in the handstand position. Each top has one leg pointing toward the center top and the other leg extended upward.

When cheerleaders are learning pyramids and other advanced stunts, they often use spotters. Spotters are there to make sure no one gets hurt while performing difficult moves. They practice so that they are always ready to stabilize, assist, and catch tops if they fall. The book, *Coaching Youth Cheerleading*, written by Varsity Brands and the American Sport Education Program, explains that spotting requires skills that do not come naturally, but can be developed with practice: "Spotting for partner stunts and pyramids requires the development of instincts that are essentially unnatural. For example, if a 100-pound object is falling toward you, your natural reaction is to move out of the way. Spotting, however, requires your squad members to move toward that object instead of away from it."[37] Trained spotters help ensure that cheerleading performances are successful and accident free.

A Strong Base

After bases take their positions, stunts and pyramids begin with the mount, when tops climb up to stand on the bases. Bases need to be strong and stable to create a firm foundation

for the tops. "Cheerleading bases are the unsung heroes of the cheerleading squad," according to writer Nicole Carlin. "Crowds will cheer as flyers [tops] are tossed into the air in complicated stunts without realizing the strength and precision that is needed to be a good cheerleading base."[38]

To provide a safe support for tops, bases use their legs and hips for stability and distribute their weight evenly over their feet, which is their base of support. By bending at the knee, cheerleaders lower their pelvis toward the ground. This lowers their center of gravity, the point at which body weight is evenly distributed. Lowering the center of gravity increases stability.

Once bases have stabilized their legs to create strong support, they take the weight of their partners on their shoulders and arms. As the tops climb up to perform, bases have to handle the pressure created by the weight of the tops. In order to maintain stability, bases push upward at the same time the tops are pushing downward.

Base cheerleaders from the UCLA practice their positioning while holding and lifting the flyers before taking the court at a basketball game.

Climbing Lightly

Most tops are small and lightweight. That makes them easier for bases to lift, support, and toss. According to Sir Isaac Newton's Second Law of Motion, the acceleration of an object depends on its mass as well as the force acting on it, small tops can also fly through the air more easily, because of their lower body mass.

As tops climb on bases to take their positions, they make physical adjustments that make them feel lighter. According to *Coaching Youth Cheerleading*, this is called "climbing lightly." In order to do this, the top pushes off the ground using one foot while the other foot is resting on the base. This takes weight off the foot being used to climb and off whichever part of the base's body that foot is resting on. At the same time, the top pushes down with his

"Cheerlebrity"
Erica Englebert

In All Star cheerleading, which allows cheerleaders to focus on training and competing rather than sideline cheering, cheerleaders start performing as preschoolers. Teenage top Erica Englebert began competing at age four. When she was eight, her mother commissioned videographer Jay Noah to make a video of Erica. She posted it on YouTube, and Erica became what Noah calls a "cheerlebrity."

"[The video] generated pages of comments from around the world, with fans wanting to know how much Erica weighed, wishing ardently that they could be her," wrote journalist Samantha Shapiro in 2011. "It wasn't long before fans ... started creating their own Erica videos, with pictures stolen from Facebook or Noah's videos. The tributes, which are typically set to love songs, show Erica, now 14, executing ever more complicated cheerleading stunts as she grows."

Samantha Shapiro. "They Grow Up So Fast." ESPN, May 12, 2011. http://sports. espn.go.com/espn/news/story?id=6120556.

or her hands on the base's shoulders. This helps to more evenly distribute the top's weight on the base until the top is in position.

Finding Balance

Once on the bases, tops need to stay balanced. If even one top in a multiperson stunt loses balance, he or she could cause the entire stunt to topple. Some of the stunts tops per-

A flyer from the University of Wisconsin uses her strength and flexibility to balance on one leg while the base holds her steadily over his head.

form require amazing balancing skills. In many partner stunts, for example, the top stands with just one foot on the base's hands. Tops use specific techniques, to maintain their balance while performing stunts.

One method tops use to maintain balance is tightening their muscles, especially core muscles. This gives tops more strength and stability and allows them to control their body positioning better. Tops also develop flexibility so they can perform with agility. They do not want to make jerky movements or abrupt weight shifts that could throw them off balance. At the same time, they also remain flexible enough to adjust to any shifting of the base beneath them by subtly adjusting their own body weight to maintain stability.

Developing methods for maintaining balance is essential for all cheerleaders. "Whether you are new to cheerleading, on the varsity squad or a professional cheerleader, balance is a key element for your sport," according to writer Roger Cahill. "Cheerleading is about performing stunts and formations that require a great deal of balance.... Improving your balance helps you become a stronger cheerleader and allows you to confidently cheer at the next level."[39]

Spectacular Dismounts

When cheerleaders dismount, or get down, from a stunt or pyramid, they often perform moves that send them flying through the air. When dismounts are executed properly, they can excite a crowd. Dramatic dismounts also incorporate a number of scientific principles. When cheerleaders perform a twisting dismount, for example, they need to overcome resistance created by gravity and friction. Gravity pulls them down toward the ground and friction caused by air molecules slows their rotation, creating an aerodynamic force called drag which opposes motion through the air. By twisting while in the air, however, cheerleaders create torque, a rotational force that helps them overcome this resistance and perform the move.

Cheerleaders also have to overcome inertia, the body's resistance to change of motion, to perform the aerial dismount. Newton's First Law of Motion states that a body in motion stays in motion until another force acts upon it. Spinning in the air requires cheerleaders to change their motion in the air. When they create torque by twisting, they create angular momentum, a force of motion that keeps the body in rotation.

While rotating during a dismount, cheerleaders can also cause their bodies to rotate faster, by pulling their arms in and crossing them over their chest. This movement lowers the body's total surface area and resistance to motion. Similarly, if they want to slow down and stop, cheerleaders can extend their arms to create more surface area and greater resistance.

Training and Conditioning

Cheerleaders train and condition specifically to improve in their positions as bases and tops. Bases need extra strength in their shoulders and legs. To build shoulder strength, they

Squats and shoulder presses are key exercises for base cheerleaders to gain the strength they need to safely perform stunts.

may do dumbbell shoulder presses. These exercises are performed by standing and holding a dumbbell in each hand. Palms face out and arms are bent at the elbow in front of the body. The cheerleader then lifts the dumbbells straight up, mimicking the way he or she needs to lift tops.

Bases and tops both exercise for leg strength using added weight when they do lunges and squats. For bases, the extra weight mimics the weight they need to be able to lift and hold. For tops, it can simply help them develop more strength. Adding weights while working out overloads muscle tissue and actually damages the tissue, but it grows as it repairs itself with new cells, becoming thicker and stronger. Young sub Kwon and Len Kravitz, who researched this process at the University of New Mexico, Albuquerque, explain, "The adaptation of muscle to the overload stress of resistance exercise begins immediately after each exercise bout, but often takes weeks or months for it to physically manifest itself. The most adaptable tissue in the human body is skeletal muscle, and it is remarkably remodeled after continuous, and carefully designed, resistance exercise training programs."[40]

Creating Flexibility and Strength

All cheerleaders need to train for flexibility and core strength. They train for flexibility with dynamic and static stretches and specific core-strengthening exercises, including crunches and V sits. V sits work the rectus abdominis, obliques, and hip flexors. They are performed by sitting with legs and back straight, then using core muscles to lift the legs to a forty-five-degree angle. At the same time, the arms reach forward toward the shins to create a deeper muscle contraction. Like weight training, this exercise challenges muscle tissue to the point of fatigue and damages it in the process. Then the tissue grows stronger and thicker as it is repaired.

In addition to these exercises, tops also focus on improving their balance while practicing their performances. They first practice their moves on the ground. While they are learning, they may use a chair to stabilize their positions. When they have mastered a move on the ground, they challenge themselves by practicing on the

Tops work to develop their balance, strength, and flexibility. They practice their moves on the ground in order to safely develop muscle memory.

edge of a curb or on a soup can. This gives them the chance to develop something known as muscle memory, without adding too much risk.

When tops develop muscle memory, new neural pathways are developed in the brain so movements become second nature. Tops need to develop muscle memory, because they cannot watch themselves making moves while in the air. Looking down at his or her own body would throw a top's alignment off balance and cause the top to fall.

The cheerleading season is year-round, so bases and tops need to train regularly all year if they want to be in top condition. In addition to strength, flexibility, and balance training, they do cardiovascular exercises, such as jogging or biking, to build slow-twitch muscles for stamina. They do plyometrics to develop fast-twitch muscles. Intense training and conditioning helps all cheerleaders to develop the muscles and skills they need to perform better. It also helps to prevent injuries. "With advanced cheerleading there is a risk of serious traumatic injuries and fractures due to falls. Jumping and landing can cause ankle and knee injuries. Wrist, elbow, and shoulder injuries can occur from repetitive quick motions," writes Nadya Swedan in an article for the Family Education Network website. "To prevent cheerleading injuries: General strengthening of the upper and lower body should be done two to three times a week. Stretching should be done daily to maintain flexibility. Balance training is helpful to prevent ankle sprains and falls."[41]

Strength and flexibility training are important, but there are also many more steps that cheerleaders can take to stay safe and injury free while competing and performing.

CHAPTER **6**

Troubles and Treatments

Today's cheerleaders are known for athletic moves, such as forming human pyramids and flipping in the air at great heights. While performing these types of movements, however, cheerleaders are at risk of being injured. In fact, cheerleading is now considered one of the most dangerous sports, with almost thirty thousand cheerleading-related emergency room visits in 2008, according to the Consumer Product Safety Commission.

Cheerleading has become more dangerous over the years, and one reason is cheerleading competitions. Cheerleaders are willing to go to extreme measures to succeed. For example, they will incorporate dangerous stunts into their routines in order to impress judges when they compete. "Since about 1999, the degree of difficulty in cheerleading has just exploded," notes Tammy Van Vleet of the Golden State Spirit Association, a California organization that trains cheerleading coaches and runs competitions. "And we're seeing elite-level gymnasts on these cheerleading squads. And not just one athlete on the floor but 35 at a time, and [the] acrobatics and stunts that they are doing … have not been matched."[42]

The dispute over recognizing cheerleading as a sport has been an obstacle to creating uniform safety measures across the United States. There are, however, cheerleading organizations that promote certain safety measures. The National Cheer Safety Foundation was created by parents who promote awareness about safety issues in cheerleading. The American Association of Cheerleading Coaches & Administrators (AACCA) has safety rules that prevent certain stunts from being performed without a spotter and that prohibit some moves altogether. The AACCA and other organizations offer safety certification programs for coaches, so they can learn to teach and supervise cheerleaders safely.

Despite the dangers, preventative measures can reduce the risks associated with cheerleading. Even when something does go wrong and a cheerleader is injured, treatments are available to resolve most problems. The process of making cheerleading safer starts when those involved take the proper safety precautions.

Safety Precautions

Coaches as well as cheerleaders can make safety a priority even before beginning a practice or performance. Clearing the cheering area is one way to begin. The cheering area needs to be free of obstacles, people, and other hazards that could cause injury, and mats should be in place to provide cushioning for cheerleaders when they perform aerial moves and dismount from stunts.

Uniforms also need to be checked for safety issues. While they may be chosen for their colors and look, they need to fit properly. If a uniform is too loose, sleeves and edges could catch on other cheerleaders' fingers. If a uniform is too tight, the cheerleader will not be able to perform moves properly, which could result in a fall or injury.

Some cheerleaders also use protective gear, which needs to be in good condition in order to be effective. Knee braces, for example, are used to prevent knee injuries caused by twisting and overextending. When worn properly, they compress ligaments to prevent inflammation. They also stabilize and cushion the knee to protect bones. A knee brace can be especially beneficial for protecting the anterior cruciate ligament (ACL), one of the four main ligaments in the knee.

A high school cheerleader has her knee wrapped in order to protect the area and prevent further injury.

Some cheerleaders wear ankle braces to support the ankles, or wrist braces to protect the wrists against twisting and hyperextension. There are even special headbands cheerleaders can wear to prevent head injuries. Some cheerleading safety advocates have even suggested that helmets be mandatory for all tops, because of the possibility of accidents during stunts and pyramids.

Environmental Dangers

When cheerleaders perform outdoors, such as during sideline cheering at a football game, there are environmental dangers to consider in addition to standard safety precautions. Cheerleaders need to take special precautions under specific environmental conditions. When the weather is hot and humid, for example, body sweat is less effective in reducing body temperature. As *Coaching Youth Cheerleading* explains, "Because the air is already saturated with water vapor (humidity), sweat doesn't evaporate as easily.... Hot, humid environments put

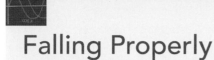

Falling Properly

Cheerleaders never want to accidentally fall when they are performing a stunt, but falling is sometimes inevitable. The best way for cheerleaders to stay safe is by learning to fall properly.

When cheerleaders know they are falling from a stunt, they shout "down!" to alert those below them. They keep their arms up and do not kick their legs or arms. Spotters are in place to catch falling tops, and mats are used to cushion a fall to the ground.

"In both gymnastics and cheerleading, learning how to fall safely is extremely important in reducing the chances for severe injuries," says Thomas J. Parr, a physician in sports medicine. "Proper falling techniques are taught in other sports and need to be a greater part of these."

Thomas J. Parr. "Cheerleading and Gymnastics." Thomas J. Parr. http://www .ftbendsportsmedicine.com/cheerleading-gymnastics.html.

squad members at risk of heat exhaustion and heatstroke."[43] Health complications, like heat cramps, heat exhaustion, and heat stroke, may come on unexpectedly and can be deadly if not properly identified and treated. Heat cramps are involuntary muscle spasms that occur when cheerleaders practice or perform for too long in hot weather. These spasms usually affect the calf, arm, abdominal, and back muscles. Treatments include resting, cooling down, drinking water or a sports drink, and gentle massage.

If heat cramps are not addressed, or the cheerleader returns to activity too soon after treating them, the cheerleader could experience heat exhaustion. Cheerleaders with heat exhaustion may perspire more and feel nauseated or lightheaded. Treatments include moving into the shade or into an air-conditioned room, loosening clothing, elevating the legs and feet slightly, drinking cool water, and spraying lightly with cool water.

The most severe heat-related illness is heat stroke. In this condition, body temperature rises to 104° F (40° C) or more.

A cheerleader suffering from heat stroke may stop perspiring, breathe rapidly, and become confused. He or she might even pass out. Treatment for heat stroke requires a visit to the emergency room to prevent damage to the brain, heart, kidneys, and muscles.

Cold weather can also be hazardous to cheerleaders. Experiencing cold weather for an extended period can result in cold-related medical issues, including frostbite and hypothermia. Frostbite occurs when tissue in parts of the body actually freezes. Symptoms include loss of feeling and color in an area of the body, usually the ears, chin, nose, cheeks, toes, or fingers. Treatments include moving to a warm room and warming the affected area with body heat or warm water.

Hypothermia occurs when the body loses heat faster than it can produce it. Body temperature drops to below 95° F (35° C). Mild hypothermia can cause confusion, but severe cases can be deadly. A cheerleader with hypothermia will need medical treatment as well as immediate first aid assistance. Treatment includes moving to a warm room, removing any wet clothing, drinking warm drinks, and warming with a blanket.

Cheerleaders can prevent frostbite and hypothermia by dressing in warm clothing when the weather is cold. They may wear warm-up pants and jackets, turtleneck body suits, sweaters, and gloves. Cheerleading attire is also available in high-tech fabric that wicks perspiration away from the body.

In addition to extreme heat and cold, cheerleaders also have to prepare for rainy weather. Proper cheerleading shoes can provide extra grip on slippery surfaces. They create friction between the ground and the cheerleader's foot to resist motion and prevent slipping. Cheerleaders may also wear clear rain jackets that keep them dry while still showing their uniform through the material.

Go, Team!

As of 2010, only thirteen states required cheerleading coaches to be certified by the American Association of Cheerleading Coaches & Administrators (AACCA).

Common Injuries

In cheerleading, many medical issues, including heat-related illnesses, can be prevented by drinking enough water to prevent dehydration. Dehydration is common in athletes and occurs when the body loses too much fluid through excessive perspiration that occurs during exercise. It can be prevented and treated by drinking small amounts of fluids throughout practices and performances.

The most common injuries in cheerleading are strains and sprains, which account for 52 percent of injuries,

ANKLE SPRAINS

Cheerleading can be a dangerous sport. A study conducted in 2006-2007 found that over half of all cheerleading injuries were sprains or strains, and the most commonly injured body part was the ankle. There are three basic types of ankle sprains: lateral inversion (the ankle rolls outward); lateral eversion (the ankle rolls inward); and high sprains (the leg twists while the foot stays planted).

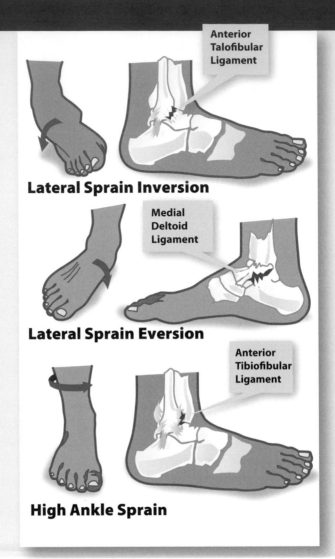

Anterior Talofibular Ligament

Lateral Sprain Inversion

Medial Deltoid Ligament

Lateral Sprain Eversion

Anterior Tibiofibular Ligament

High Ankle Sprain

but fractures, concussions, and minor cuts and scrapes are often reported as well. A strain occurs when muscles or tendons, fibrous cords of tissue connecting muscle to bone, tear. It may cause muscle spasms. A sprain occurs when ligaments are stretched or torn. It may cause bruising. Cheerleaders sometimes hear or feel a "pop" in their joint when the injury occurs. Both strains and sprains cause pain and swelling and limit a cheerleader's ability to move. Depending on the ligaments involved and the extent of the injury, strains and sprains can be traumatic and debilitating. Bethany Hancock was a senior in high school when she tore the anterior cruciate ligaments in both knees while practicing a difficult cheerleading jump. "It was the worst pain ever," she said. "I bounced off the floor and I could feel shock waves run up my legs, and I lay there and screamed."[44]

For mild strains and sprains, treatment can take place at home. Cheerleaders can take over-the-counter medications to reduce pain. They can elevate the injured area above heart level to prevent blood from pooling at the injury site. They can also use ice to reduce swelling. Authors William C. Shiel Jr. and Leslie J. Schoenfield explain why the use of ice works:

> The swelling and much of the inflammation that follows an injury is largely due to the leakage of blood from the ruptured capillaries. Therefore, cold applications with ice can help by causing the blood vessels to constrict (clamp down). This constriction of the blood vessels prevents further leakage of blood and serum and minimizes swelling and pain. The cold from an ice pack application also has an added benefit of providing pain relief.[45]

In most cases, strains and sprains heal with rest. In some cases, however, they require medical treatment. Hancock had two surgeries to repair her torn ligaments and spent much of a year in treatment and recovery. She was left with permanent damage that prevented her from cheering at the college level.

Less severe injuries, such as bruises, which show through the skin when blood leaks from broken capillaries and pools in an area, benefit from similar ice treatment. Fractures, meanwhile, require medical treatment to set the bone and hold it in place for proper healing.

Go, Team!

In 2010, the American Association of Cheerleading Coaches & Administrators (AACCA) created new safety rules that banned basket tosses and double full twisting dismounts for all elementary, middle school, and junior high cheerleaders.

Catastrophic Injuries

Catastrophic cheerleading injuries are uncommon, but they do happen. They include injuries such as severe fractures and concussions, which cheerleaders may not recover from completely. They also include injuries that result in paralysis or death.

Laura Jackson was a high school cheerleader in 2003 when she attempted a back flip and landed on her head. She fractured her neck and damaged her spinal cord, which left her paralyzed from the neck down and in need of a ventilator to breathe. In 2010 journalist Melissa Dahl wrote, "Seven years after Laura's accident, the Jacksons try not to dwell on all the what-ifs: What if a trained coach had been there to catch Laura when she attempted her back flip, instead of a teen girl? Or what if the tumbling moves took place on a springboard surface—like gymnasts perform on—rather than a thin wrestling mat on a wooden gymnasium floor?"[46]

Another high school cheerleader, Ashley Burns, died in 2005 while performing an arabesque double down. In this stunt, a top performs a double-down dismount by completing two twists in the air before being caught by the bases below. Instead of completing the second twist, however, Ashley fell onto another cheerleader and injured her spleen. She died on the way to the hospital. Nicole Weisensee Egan, a writer for People magazine, writes,

> [Burns's mother] filed a wrongful death lawsuit against the East Elite Cheer Gym in Tewksbury, Mass., where her daughter died because, among other reasons, there was no emergency plan in place. "An emergency plan is something as simple as 'These are the signs you need to look out for, and if this happens, ... call 911,'" says her attorney Robert Bonsignore. "This was 100 percent preventable. If they'd gotten her to the hospital in time, she would be alive."[47]

With cheerleading becoming increasingly dangerous, advocates and cheerleading organizations are hoping that improved safety guidelines will prevent the kinds of accidents that happened to Laura and Ashley.

Steroids

Most injuries in cheerleading are due to accidents. Other types of health problems can arise, however, when cheerleaders use substances, such as anabolic steroids, to help improve their performance. Anabolic steroids are synthetic hormones that promote muscle growth. They can be taken orally, injected through the skin, or massaged into the skin as a cream. Doctors prescribe anabolic steroids to treat

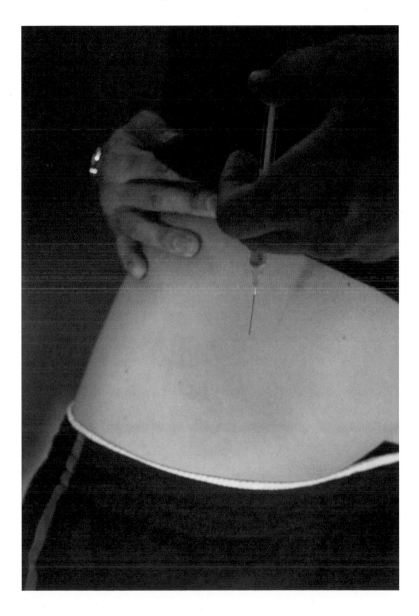

Despite the dangers, some cheerleaders have resorted to using steroids to improve their performance.

conditions such as delayed puberty and body wasting (a condition that causes loss of weight and muscle tissue), but they do not normally prescribe them to enhance athletic performance. In fact, that is illegal because anabolic steroid use is risky and creates unfair advantages for athletes who use them. Still, many athletes can get anabolic steroids from doctors, trainers, coaches or friends with a prescription.

When steroids are abused, they can cause negative physical side effects. According to the National Drug Intelligence Center, "physical consequences include liver tumors and cancer, jaundice, high blood pressure and increases in cholesterol levels, kidney tumors, fluid retention, and severe acne. Individuals who are still growing (adolescents) risk prematurely halting their growth because of early skeletal maturation and acceleration of puberty."[48]

In addition to physical problems, psychological problems can develop as a result of steroid use. Steriods can cause dramatic mood swings, violent behavior, depression, paranoia, extreme irritability, and impaired judgment. High school cheerleader Dionne Passacantando, for instance, began using steroids at seventeen years old. Two weeks later, she was feeling isolated. She started having intense mood swings and eventually began having suicidal thoughts. "Near the end of it, I had a fight with my parents and even went to such extremes to go into our medicine cabinet and just grab a lot of over the counter pills," she said in an interview. "I was angry and I guess just kind of towards a breaking point, feeling kind of suicidal."[49]

Despite these possible repercussions, cheerleaders, and other athletes, still occasionally turn to steroids in an attempt to improve their performance even though they are dangerous and illegal without a prescription.

Eating Disorders

Cheerleaders may also risk their health by trying to lose too much weight in the hope of improving their performance. Some cheerleaders, mainly tops who want to be as light as possible, develop eating disorders, such as anorexia nervosa or bulimia. People with anorexia nervosa obsess about how

The pressure on cheerleaders, especially flyers, to keep their weight in check can lead to eating disorders that can result in both physical and psychological damage.

much they eat and how much they weigh. They severely limit their nutritional intake, use laxatives to avoid weight gain, and may exercise excessively to burn calories. On the other hand, individuals who are bulimic do eat food, often excessive amounts of food, but will induce vomiting after a meal in an attempt to lose weight.

Anorexia nervosa and bulimia may be caused by a combination of biological, sociocultural, and psychological issues. According to the Mayo Clinic, anorexia nervosa is likely brought on by a variety of factors, including a predisposition, or genetic vulnerability, toward "perfectionism, sensitivity and perseverance."[50] Anorexia nervosa may also be caused by certain levels of serotonin, a brain chemical linked with depression, or peer pressure to be thin.

If untreated, these disorders can lead to starvation and death. There are also emotional problems associated with eating disorders, including intense fear of gaining weight and a distorted body image.

While some cheerleaders suffer from psychological problems or develop them through engaging in harmful behavior, most cheerleaders are psychologically healthy. They also have certain psychological traits as a group that make them successful in cheerleading.

CHAPTER **7**

The Psychology of Cheerleading

Cheerleaders are known for being upbeat, positive, and mentally strong. Some cheerleaders seem to come by these traits naturally. Even cheerleaders who have been catastrophically injured have demonstrated a positive attitude. Laura Jackson, for example, who was paralyzed from the neck down in a cheerleading accident in 2003, said this about her life after cheering: "I still watch it on ESPN all the time—I watch all the cheer competitions. I love going to a game to watch the cheerleaders. But it's hard not having it in my life. I'm still like a cheerleader at heart—I'm still happy and I'm still hyper. It's just always going to be a part of me."[51]

Similarly, in 2006, college cheerleader Kristi Yamaoka fell 15 feet (4.6m) from a human pyramid and landed on her head. She suffered a concussion, a spinal fracture, and a bruised lung. Still, she continued to cheer as paramedics carried her away on a stretcher by moving her arms to the beat of the music. "My biggest concern was that I didn't want my squad to be distracted—so that they could continue cheering on the team—and I didn't want my team to be distracted from winning the game," she said later in an interview. "I'm still a cheerleader—on a stretcher or not. So as soon as I heard that fight song, I knew my job and just started to do my thing."[52]

Southern Illinois University cheerleader Kristi Yamaoka raises her arms to perform the movements of a cheer as she is removed from the court on a stretcher after falling on her head from the top of a pyramid.

It is difficult to know whether cheerleaders are born with certain upbeat personality traits that make them suited for cheerleading, but some studies show that personality traits are inherited. "The genetic makeup of a child is a stronger influence on personality than child rearing, according to the first study to examine identical twins reared in different families. The findings shatter a widespread belief among experts and laymen alike in the primacy of family influence and are sure to engender fierce debate,"[53] writes journalist Daniel Goleman. Life experience also plays a role in shaping personality. Regardless of their genetic makeup and life experience, all cheerleaders must work to develop and strengthen the psychological qualities they need to succeed when performing and competing.

Coping with Stress

While cheering, dancing, performing stunts, and competing are enjoyable activities for cheerleaders, they can also be stressful activities. Stress refers to the body's physical

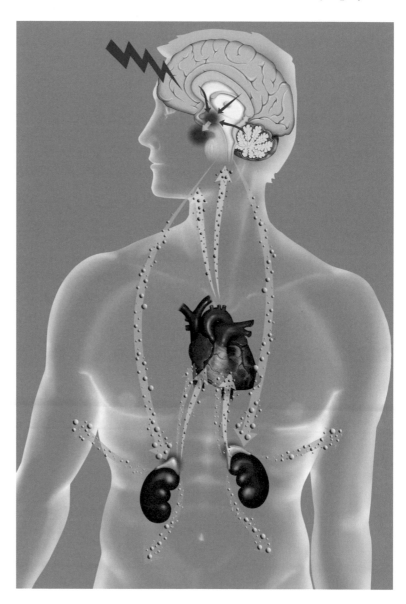

An illustration shows how the body reacts to stress. The adrenal glands release cortisol (blue arrows) and adrenaline (yellow arrows), which affect the brain and heart.

and emotional responses to outside events. When a person is stressed, the adrenal glands release adrenaline, which increases breathing rate, heart rate, and blood pressure. Blood circulates more quickly to the brain and muscles, so the senses become heightened and perception of pain decreases. The adrenal glands also release cortisol, which creates a quick burst of energy as well as increasing memory function and immunity. Stress can also cause a range of emotions, from anger and irritability to extreme excitement and confidence.

Often, stress is related to negative experiences. People become stressed when they are overloaded with work or confronted with challenges they do not know how to handle. When cheerleaders perform, they may feel pressure to do well and not make mistakes. They may worry about getting injured or reinjured.

Stress can also be a response to positive experiences, however. Even when cheerleaders are not worrying before a performance, they may feel the physical effects of positive stress, or eustress. Positive stress can inspire cheerleaders to practice more and become better prepared. This can lead cheerleaders to feel more confident about their abilities.

While some stress can be good, too much stress over a period of time is never healthy. "Chronic stress can affect both our physical and psychological well-being by causing a variety of problems including anxiety, insomnia, muscle

Two Kinds of Smiles

There are two kinds of smiles: real and fake. "When someone smiles out of genuine delight, a facial muscle called the orbicularis oculi involuntary contracts, crinkling the skin around the eyes," writes journalist Jennifer Margulis. "Most of us are incapable of deliberately moving this muscle, which means that when a person fakes a smile, her orbicularis oculi likely won't budge."

Jennifer Margulis. "The State of the Smile." *O, The Oprah Magazine*, August 2011.

pain, high blood pressure and a weakened immune system," according to the American Psychological Association. "Research shows that stress can contribute to the development of major illnesses, such as heart disease, depression and obesity. The consequences of chronic stress are serious."[54] Because cheerleaders encounter stressful events on a regular basis—each time they perform or compete—they need to learn how to cope with stress so it does not become a chronic condition.

One method many athletes use to cope with stress is mental imagery. If they are nervous about a game or routine, then before they perform, they imagine themselves in detail, performing well. According to writer Annie Plessinger,

> the reason visual imagery works lies in the fact that when you imagine yourself perform to perfection and doing precisely what you want, you are in turn physiologically creating neural patterns in your brain, just as if you had physically performed the action. These patterns are similar to small tracks engraved in the brain cells, which can ultimately enable an athlete to perform physical feats by simply mentally practicing the move. Hence, mental imagery is intended to train our minds and create the neural patterns in our brain to teach our muscles to do exactly what we want them to do.[55]

Completing a performance mentally beforehand can reinforce the athlete's memory of the motions needed to be successful, while also relieving anxiety.

Cheerleaders also cope with stress by regulating the physical changes stress causes in their bodies. For example, they may practice deep breathing to slow their breathing rate. They may also practice muscle relaxation, by contracting and releasing their muscles. This can reduce muscle tension. According to the Mayo Clinic,

> in general, relaxation techniques involve refocusing your attention on something calming and increasing awareness of your body.... Once you know what the stress response feels like, you can make a conscious

effort to practice a relaxation technique the moment you start to feel stress symptoms. This can prevent stress from spiraling out of control … relaxation techniques are skills. And as with any skill, your ability to relax improves with practice.[56]

Positive Thinking

Another way cheerleaders reduce stress is through positive thinking. In order to project a positive outer attitude, cheerleaders must have a positive inner attitude. They develop this attitude by thinking positive thoughts.

To develop a habit of positive thinking, cheerleaders use quotes or affirmations to keep their focus upbeat. They replace negative self-talk with positive self-talk. They accept negative emotions so they can be open to positive ones. They look for the best in difficult situations. They try not to

A group of cheerleaders project their positive inner attitudes through their smiles and enthusiasm. Positive thinking helps cheerleaders reduce stress and remain energetic.

complain. They relabel challenges as opportunities, so they can face them head on. Over time, these mental approaches to life can become a habit.

When habits are formed, neural pathways are formed in the brain. These pathways make positive thinking more natural and less of an effort. Positive thinking also activates the brain's left prefrontal cortex. Researchers have found that activating the left prefrontal cortex leads to a stronger immune system response in the body, which fights off disease and helps to keep the body healthy. In this way, a positive attitude can help cheerleaders with their athletic performance. Their mental training can make them physically stronger. Journalist Sharon Jason writes,

Positive thinking and a positive attitude may indeed have power. That belief has long been conjecture, but in recent years scientists studying the mind-body connection are finding that an optimistic outlook can improve

Science of Resilience

Resilient people, like top athletes, can perform well under stress. They rise to physical challenges even when their interoceptive sense, which indicates the body's internal state, tells them to rest. There is evidence that resilience comes, in part, from certain advantages in an individual's brain.

"Individuals who shine in tough circumstances may benefit from highly attuned interoception, which then informs the decision-making areas of the brain," according to *Scientific American* blogger Sandra Upson. "Interoception is thought to rely heavily on the insula, a small brain area that plays an important role in self-awareness and emotional experiences." Individuals who are able to persevere despite challenges may do well in activities like cheerleading, which promote positive thinking and outgoing attitudes.

Sandra Upson. "Can Extreme Resilience Be Taught?" *Scientific American*, November 16, 2011. http://blogs.scientificamerican.com/observations/2011/11/16/can-extreme-resilience-be-taught/.

more than just mental health.... [Carol Ryff, a psychology professor at the University of Wisconsin-Madison,] has shown that individuals with higher levels of well-being have lower cardiovascular risk, lower levels of stress hormones and lower levels of inflammation, which serves as a marker of the immune system.[57]

Just like other people, cheerleaders experience a range of emotions. They cannot always be happy and in good spirits. Cheerleaders make extra efforts, however, to look on the bright side and offer words of encouragement even in negative situations. Cheerleader Ryan Martin writes,

You know those crazy, easily excited, extremely positive people that can sometimes be a little bit annoying? We all have them in our lives and even though sometimes we just want to hear one negative word come out of their mouths, their positive, encouraging words can make a huge difference in our lives. I consider myself one of these people due to the fact that I grew up in cheerleading.... As a cheerleader I feel like I have been taught to see the best in every situation—or at least fake it![58]

Crowd Behavior

Maintaining a positive outlook is one way cheerleaders influence crowd behavior so their audience will stay in control and positive about their team. "Cheerleaders don't always get to cheer for a winning team," points out former college cheerleader Maria Sfreddo. "Unlike players who throw their helmets in frustration when their opponent gains a hefty lead, cheerleaders must stay positive. In these situations, they pull out the big guns, like complex tumbling passes and dangerous stunts. It's not easy to get a stadium full of disenchanted fans to yell along with you while they watch their team die a slow death, but that never stopped us from trying."[59]

Cheerleaders also use visual cues to influence crowd behavior for positive results. One technique they use is a

Cheerleaders use happy facial expressions and gestures to prompt the crowd to remain interested in the game, even when their team is losing.

friendly, open facial expression. Cheerleaders are encouraged to practice smiling when they rehearse because during performances, they should always smile. "Cheerleaders are known for their smiles," according to Confident Cheerleading, a website that offers cheerleading tips. "At tryouts, the judges will notice if you are connecting to the audience (the judges) and if you are smiling."[60]

Smiling helps cheerleaders connect with their audience because a happy expression inspires those who see it to mimic it. Writer Eric Jaffe explains,

A smile begins in our sensory corridors.... This emotional data funnels to the brain, exciting the left anterior temporal region in particular, then smolders to the surface of the face, where two muscles, standing at attention, are roused into action: The zygomatic major, which resides in the cheek, tugs the lips upward, and the orbicularis oculi, which encircles the eye socket, squeezes the outside corners into the shape of a crow's foot. The entire event is short—typically lasting from two-thirds of a second to four seconds—and those who witness it often respond by mirroring the action, and smiling back.[61]

Smiling back makes the people mimicking the smile feel good. Research has shown that smiling can make a person happier and even reduce pain. "It would appear that the way we feel emotions isn't just restricted to our brain—there are parts of our bodies that help and reinforce the feelings we're having," says Michael Lewis, a coauthor of a study on how emotions are reinforced. "It's like a feedback loop."[62]

Cheerleaders also use auditory cues when they chant and cheer to influence a crowd's behavior. Some cheerleading chants require a response, which directs audience attention. Chanting and cheering also help synchronize behavior, which inspires a psychological response in crowds. It helps to bond individuals toward a common goal. Journalist Jeffrey Kluger explains,

> Human beings are naturally skilled at forming groups and communities—which is a very good thing if you want to call yourself a social species. But we often need a little help to find our interpersonal rhythm, and it often comes in ways that involve literal rhythm. Soldiers march and chant. Religions incorporate singing and even dancing in their rituals. Sports events are filled with songs, synchronized cheers, and cries of "DEE-fense." … The closeness that comes from cheering and rooting together often stays with you when you leave the stadium.[63]

In addition, cheerleaders use the skills they have developed as athletes to influence crowd behavior. By dancing well and performing dramatic stunts, they can keep an audience interested even during breaks in a game or when a game is not going well. Capturing the audience's attention is perhaps the most critical aspect of a cheerleader's job. Once cheerleaders have that attention, they have an opportunity to show off what they can do. It is their chance to prove themselves true athletes.

NOTES

Chapter 1: Transformation of Cheerleading

1. Katie Thomas. "Born on Sideline, Cheering Clamors to Be Sport." *New York Times*, May 22, 2011. http:// www.nytimes.com/2011/05/23/ sports/gender-games-born-on-sideline-cheering-clamors-to-be-sport.html?pagewanted=1&_ r=3&ref=sports.

2. Quoted in John Branch. "Shaking Pompoms for the Grandfather of Modern Cheerleading." *New York Times*, March 14, 2009. http:// www.nytimes.com/2009/03/15/ sports/ncaabasketball/15cheer .html?pagewanted=all.

3. Branch. "Shaking Pompoms for the Grandfather of Modern Cheerleading."

4. Quoted in Diane Macedo. "Judges Ruling Sparks National Debate over Cheerleading: Sport or No Sport?" Fox News, July 22, 2010. http:// www.foxnews.com/us/2010/07/22/ judges-ruling-sparks-national-debate-chearleading-sport-sport/.

5. Macedo. "Judges Ruling Sparks National Debate over Cheerleading."

6. Quoted in Associated Press, "Cheering Could Become NCAA Sport." September 8, 2010. http:// sports.espn.go.com/ncaa/news/ story?id=5546963

7. Quoted in "Varsity Weighs In on Cheerleading as Sport Debate." Varsity.com, June 22, 2010. http:// varsity.com/event/1378/varsity-weighs-in-on-cheerleading-as-sport-debate.aspx.

8. Thomas. "Born on Sideline, Cheering Clamors to Be Sport."

Chapter 2: Chants and Cheers

9. Sara Ipatenco. "Cheerleading Skills Checklist." Livestrong.com, June 6, 2011. http://www.livestrong.com/ article/464523-cheerleading-skills-checklist/.

10. Jami Kastner. "Cheerleading Cheers, Chants & Routines." Livestrong. com, June 14, 2011. http://www .livestrong.com/article/356214-cheerleading-cheers-chants-rou tines/.

11. Kastner. "Cheerleading Cheers, Chants & Routines."

12. "The Anatomy & Physiology of Voice." Voice Academy. http:// www.uiowa.edu/~shcvoice/science .html.

13. "The Anatomy & Physiology of Voice."

14. Cristina Lianchic. "Want to Be a Cheerleader? Dominate with Perfect Diet & Training!" Body-building.com, September 2, 2008. http://www.bodybuilding.com/fun/cheerleader_training.htm.

15. "Vocal Warm Ups." The Voice and Swallowing Institute, The New York Eye and Ear Infirmary, New York, NY.

16. "Vocal Warm Ups."

17. "Singers and Other Professional Voice Users." Lions Voice Clinic. http://www.lionsvoiceclinic.umn.edu/page4.htm.

Chapter 3: Dance Moves

18. Chris Callaway. "Differences Between Cheerleading and Dance." Livestrong.com, June 15, 2011. http://www.livestrong.com/article/471166-differences-between-cheerleading-dance/.

19. Quoted in Daniel J. DeNoon. "Complex Muscle Movements: Learn by Watching." WebMD, April 6, 2005. http://www.webmd.com/fitness-exercise/news/20050406/complex-muscle-movements-learn-by-watching.

20. Virginia Wilmerding, and Donna Krasnow. "Motor Learning and Teaching Dance." International Association for Dance Medicine & Science. http://www.iadms.org/displaycommon.cfm?an=1&subarticlenbr=250.

21. Wilmerding, and Krasnow. "Motor Learning and Teaching Dance."

22. Jami Kastner. "What Exercises Do Competitive Cheerleaders Do?" Livestrong.com, July 24, 2011. http://www.livestrong.com/article/499961-what-exercises-do-competitive-cheerleaders-do/.

23. Julie Anne Sommers and Active Team Sports. "Leg Exercises for Cheerleaders." Active.com. http://www.active.com/cheerleading/Articles/Leg_exercises_for_cheerleaders.htm.

24. Dan Harriman. "Which Are Better: Squats or Lunges?" Livestrong.com, May 26, 2011. http://www.livestrong.com/article/343944-which-are-better-squats-or-lunges/.

25. Alexis Kragenbrink Jenkins. "What Exercises Strengthen Feet for Dancing?" Livestrong.com, July 8, 2011. http://www.livestrong.com/article/487797-what-exercises-strengthen-feet-for-dancing/.

26. Jenkins. "What Exercises Strengthen Feet for Dancing?"

27. Elizabeth Quinn. "Exercise Science Principles of Conditioning." About.com, August 15, 2011. http://sportsmedicine.about.com/od/training/a/Ex-Science.htm.

28. Quoted in Claudia Dreifus. "Exploring Music's Hold on the Mind." New York Times, May 31, 2010. http://www.nytimes.com/2010/06/01/science/01conv.html?partner=rss&emc=rss.

29. Steven Brown, and Lawrence M. Parsons. "So You Think You Can

Dance?: PET Scans Reveal Your Brain's Inner Choreography." *Scientific American*, June 16, 2008. http://www.scientificamerican.com/article.cfm?id=the-neuroscience-of-dance.

30. Quoted in Victoria Gill. "Singing 'Rewires' Damaged Brain." BBC News, February 21, 2010. http://news.bbc.co.uk/2/hi/8526699.stm.

31. Carolyn Butler. "Science Behind 'Feel Good' Music." azcentral.com, March 10, 2011. http://www.azcentral.com/arizonarepublic/arizonaliving/articles/2011/03/10/20110310musichealth0310.html.

Chapter 4: Tumbling and Jumping

32. Kindra Harvey. "Physics of Cheerleading." Livestrong.com, July 26, 2011. http://www.livestrong.com/article/502528-physics-of-cheerleading/.

33. Selene Yeager. "The Secret to Being Fit for Life: Muscle Memory." *Women's Health*, December 2010. http://www.womenshealthmag.com/fitness/fit-for-life?page=2.

34. Jami Kastner. "Different Cheerleading Positions." Livestrong.com, June 8, 2011. http://www.livestrong.com/article/466359-different-cheerleading-positions/.

35. Graig White. "Hard Core Stability." American Cheer Express. http://www.americancheer.com/images/fitness/fitness.htm.

Chapter 5: Stunts and Pyramids

36. "Stunting." Cheer Place. http://cheerplace.tripod.com/stunting/.

37. Varsity Brands and American Sport Education Program. *Coaching Youth Cheerleading*. Champaign, IL: Human Kinetics, p. 64.

38. Nicole Carlin. "How to Properly Base in Cheerleading." Livestrong.com, June 28, 2011. http://www.livestrong.com/article/481105-how-to-properly-base-in-cheerleading/.

39. Roger Cahill. "How to Get Better Balance for Cheerleading." Livestrong.com, July 30, 2011. http://www.livestrong.com/article/505536-how-to-get-better-balance-for-cheerleading/.

40. Young sub Kwon, and Len Kravitz. "How Do Muscles Grow?" University of New Mexico, http://www.unm.edu/~lkravitz/Article%20folder/musclesgrowLK.html.

41. Nadya Swedan. "Sports-Specific Injuries." Family Education Network, 2003. http://life.familyeducation.com/sports/wounds-and-injuries/36044.html.

Chapter 6: Troubles and Treatments

42. Quoted in Lisa Ling, and Arash Ghadishah. "Most Dangerous Sport of All May Be Cheerleading." ABC News, January 4, 2010. http://abcnews.go.com/Nightline/cheer

leading-dangerous-sport-young-girls/story?id=9473938.

43. Varsity Brands and American Sport Education Program. *Coaching Youth Cheerleading*, p. 30.

44. Quoted in Heather Cabot. "Cheerleading Injuries on the Rise." ABC News, January 3, 2006. http://abcnews.go.com/GMA/Health/story?id=1465814

45. William C. Shiel Jr., and Leslie J. Schoenfield. "Ice or Heat—'Which Should I Apply?'" MedicineNet.com. http://www.medicinenet.com/script/main/art.asp?articlekey=18347.

46. Melissa Dahl. "Flying Without a Net: Cheer Injuries on the Rise." MSNBC.com, May 20, 2010. http://www.msnbc.msn.com/id/37020978/ns/health-fitness/t/flying-without-net-cheer-injuries-rise/.

47. Nicole Weisensee Egan. "Is Cheering Safe?" *People*, January 19, 2009. http://www.people.com/people/archive/article/0,,20252121,00.html.

48. "Steroid Fast Facts." National Drug Intelligence Center. http://www.justice.gov/ndic/pubs5/5448/.

49. Quoted in "Cheerleader Drawn to Steroids." ABC News, February, 20, 2008. http://abcnews.go.com/GMA/video?id=4315779.

50. "Anorexia Nervosa: Causes." Mayo Clinic. http://www.mayoclinic.com/health/anorexia/DS00606/DSECTION=causes.

Chapter 7: The Psychology of Cheerleading

51. Quoted in Dahl. "Flying Without a Net."

52. Quoted in Associated Press. "Cheerleader Worried for Team, Not Herself." NBC Sports, March 8, 2006. http://nbcsports.msnbc.com/id/11699607/.

53. Daniel Goleman. "Major Personality Study Finds That Personality Traits Are Mostly Inherited." *New York Times*, December 2, 1986.

54. "Stress Won't Go Away? Maybe You Are Suffering from Chronic Stress." American Psychological Association. http://www.apa.org/helpcenter/chronic-stress.aspx.

55. Annie Plessinger. "The Effects of Mental Imagery on Athletic Performance." Vanderbilt University Psychology Department. http://www.vanderbilt.edu/ans/psychology/health_psychology/mentalimagery.html.

56. "Stress Management: Relaxation Techniques." Mayo Clinic. http://www.mayoclinic.com/health/relaxation-technique/SR00007.

57. Sharon Jayson. "Power of a Super Attitude." *USA Today*, October 12, 2004. http://www.usatoday.com/news/health/2004-10-12-mind-body_x.htm.

58. Ryan Martin. "Staying Positive—Even in Tough Times." America Needs Cheerleaders, March 24, 2011. http://americaneedscheerleaders.com/life-beyond-cheer/

staying-positive-%E2%80%93-even-in-tough-times.html.

59. Maria Sfreddo. "Why Cheerleaders Make Good Lawyers." Around the Water Cooler, July 12, 2011. http://h20cooler.wordpress.com/2011/07/12/why-cheerleaders-make-good-lawyers/.

60. "At Cheerleading Tryouts—Smile!" Confident Cheerleading. http://www.confidentcheerleadingblog.com/tryouts/at-cheerleading-tryouts-smile/.

61. Eric Jaffe. "The Psychological Study of Smiling." Association for Psychological Science, December 2010. http://www.psychologicalscience.org/index.php/publications/observer/the-psychological-study-of-smiling.html.

62. Quoted in Melinda Wenner. "Smile! It Could Make You Happier." *Scientific American*, October 14, 2009. http://www.scientificamerican.com/article.cfm?id=smile-it-could-make-you-happier.

63. Jeffrey Kluger. "What Sports Fans Get from Chanting and Cheering." *Time*, February 1, 2009. http://www.time.com/time/health/article/0,8599,1876065,00.html.

agility: An ability to move with speed and skill.

axis of rotation: The center point or line around which a rotating object spins.

cell: The smallest unit of an organism that functions independently.

center of gravity: An imaginary point in an object where the total weight of the object is concentrated.

cerebellum: The part of the brain that coordinates voluntary muscular movement and maintains the body's balance and posture.

drag: Resistance caused by air flow.

dynamic stretching: A method of stretching muscles that includes moving them through a joint's range of motion.

fast-twitch fibers: Muscle fibers that contract more quickly and can grow larger than slow-twitch fibers but have less endurance.

force: Any outside stress that causes an object to move or change its shape.

friction: Resistance to motion caused when two objects touch.

gravity: The force of attraction between all objects that have mass.

hypothermia: Abnormally low body temperature.

inertia: The tendency of a moving object to remain in motion or a still object to remain at rest unless acted on by an outside force.

inflammation: A condition in which body tissue becomes red and swollen.

kinetic energy: The form of energy involved in movement.

ligament: A band of tissue connecting bones at a joint.

mass: The amount of matter in an object.

molecule: The smallest unit of a substance that exists independently.

momentum: A measure of how an object moves, depending on its mass and velocity. The equation is momentum (p) = mass (m) x velocity (v).

pitch: The high or low quality of a tone, determined by the vibrations causing it.

plyometrics: A method of power training that puts the muscles in a pre-stretch before executing a powerful contraction.

potential energy: Energy stored in an object because of its position.

proprioception: A sense of one's body in space.

slow-twitch fibers: A type of muscle fibers that contracts slower and does not grow as large as fast-twitch fibers but have more endurance.

static stretching: Stretching a muscle with a slow movement and holding the stretch for twenty to thirty seconds.

tendon: A band of tissue attaching muscle to bone.

torque: A twisting force applied to a body or object.

velocity: A measure of the rate of change in position over a period of time in a particular direction.

wavelength: The distance between two points on successive waves.

FOR MORE INFORMATION

Books

Linda Rae Chappell. *Coaching Cheerleading Successfully*. Champaign, IL: Human Kinetics, 2005. An instructional book about how to coach cheerleading.

Kate Torgovnick. *Cheer! Inside the Secret World of College Cheerleaders*. New York: Touchstone, 2009. An inside look at cheerleading that follows cheerleaders from three competing colleges.

Internet Sources

Lisa Ling, and Arash Ghadishah. "Most Dangerous 'Sport' of All May Be Cheerleading." ABC News, January 4, 2010. http://abcnews.go.com/Nightline/cheerleading-dangerous-sport-young-girls/story?id=9473938.

Samantha Shapiro. "They Grow Up So Fast." ESPN, May 12, 2011. http://sports.espn.go.com/espn/news/story?id=6120556.

Katie Thomas. "Born on Sideline, Cheering Clamors to Be Sport." *New York Times*, May 22, 2011. http://www.nytimes.com/2011/05/23/sports/gender games-born-on-sideline-cheering-clamors-to-be-sport.html?pagewanted=1&_r=3&ref=sports.

Websites

American Association of Cheerleading Coaches & Administrators (http://aacca.org). This organization provides education, safety training, and certification for cheerleading coaches.

National Cheerleading Association (http://nca.varsity.com). This organization sponsors nationwide cheerleading camps and competitions.

Voice Academy (www.uiowa.edu/~shcvoice). This site, maintained by the National Center for Voice & Speech at the University of Utah, explains the scientific process of making vocal sounds.

INDEX

Momentum, 50
Mood swings, 80
Motion, laws of, 50, 65
Motor learning, 32, *33*, 34–36
Muscle memory, 47–48
Music, 13–14, 41, *43*, 43–44

N

National Cheer Safety Foundation, 71
National Cheerleaders Association, 13
National Collegiate Athletic
    Association, 18
National Collegiate Athletics and
    Tumbling Association, 18
National Football League, 16
Newton, Isaac, 50

O

Observation, 32, 34

P

Paralysis, 78, 82
Parr, Thomas J., 73
Partner stunts. *See* Stunts and
    pyramids
Passacantando, Dionne, 80
Patel, Aniruddh D., 38, 41, 43–44, 65
Personality, 82–84
Phonation, 24–25
Physics
    back tucks, *52*
    dismounts, 64–65
    jumps, 49–51, 53–54
    landing, 54–55
    tumbling, 45, *46*, 47
Physiotherapists, 34

Plyometrics, 56
Pom-poms, 11–12
Popularity, international, 15–16
Positive thinking, 82–84, 87–89,
    89–90
Princeton University, 9
Proprioception, 35, 48
Props, 11–12
Protective gear, 71–72, *72*
Psychology
    crowd behavior, 89–91, *90*
    eating disorders, 80–81
    positive thinking, 82–84, 87–89
    steroid use, 80
    stress, coping with, *84*, 84–87
Puberty, 21
Pyramids. *See* Stunts and pyramids

Q

Quinnipiac College, 17

R

Rain, 75
Repetition, 35–36, 40–41
Replication, 34–35
Resilience, 88
Respiratory system, *23*, 23–24
Rest, 53
Rotation, *46*, 47, 65–66

S

Safety, 56, 70–72, *72*, 77
Second Law of Motion, 50
Seely, Bill, 18
Self talk, 87
Sfreddo, Maria, 89

PICTURE CREDITS

ABOUT THE AUTHOR

Heather E. Schwartz writes frequently about sports and science. She lives in upstate New York with her husband and son.

DATE DUE

			PRINTED IN U.S.A.